Kidnapped

When I looked round the ship I saw a furnace boiling on the deck, and many black people all chained together, every one of their faces full of sorrow. Soon the men who had brought me on board went off the ship, and left me abandoned to despair. I had no chance now of returning to my country—and not even the smallest chance of getting back to shore.

Nearly every day some of my companions were brought upon deck at the point of death. I hoped that I would soon die too. Often I thought that the inhabitants of the deep were much happier than I. I envied the fish their freedom, and I wished I could have changed my lot for theirs.

Also by Ann Cameron:

The Stories Julian Tells

More Stories Julian Tells

The Stories Huey Tells

More Stories Huey Tells

The Most Beautiful Place in the World

The
Kidnapped Prince
The Life of Olaudah Equiano

By
Olaudah Equiano

Adapted by
Ann Cameron

With an introduction
by Henry Louis Gates, Jr.

A Knopf Paperback
Alfred A. Knopf
New York

A KNOPF PAPERBACK PUBLISHED BY ALFRED A. KNOPF, INC.

Copyright © 1995 by Ann Cameron
Introduction copyright © 1995 by Henry Louis Gates, Jr.
Cover art copyright © 1995 by Dan Andreasen
Map copyright © 1995 by Rodica Prato

www.randomhouse.com/kids

Library of Congress Cataloging-in-Publication Data
Cameron, Ann
The kidnapped prince : the life of Olaudah Equiano / adapted by Ann Cameron ; introduction by Henry Louis Gates, Jr.
p.   cm.
Adaptation of: The interesting narrative of the life of Olaudah Equiano. Includes bibliographical references.
1. Equiano, Olaudah, b. 1745—Juvenile literature. 2. Slaves—Biography—Juvenile literature. I. Equiano, Olaudah, b. 1745. Interesting narrative of the life of Olaudah Equiano. II. Title. III. Title: Life of Olaudah Equiano.
HT869.E6C36   1994   305.5'67—dc20   93-29914
[B]

ISBN   0-375-80346-7 (pbk.)

First Knopf Paperback edition: January 2000
Printed in the United States of America

10 9 8 7 6 5 4 3 2 1

Contents

INTRODUCTION

Olaudah Equiano was an African boy—a prince who was kidnapped and carried off to a strange new world. Under its cruel laws he was legally nothing more than another man's property, with no right to decide the course of his life or to protest anything that was done to him.

What is remarkable is that under these oppressive conditions he survived—without losing his sanity, integrity, or sense of humor. Before gaining his freedom, he received a wide and varied education and became one of the best-traveled people of his time. The history of his life is an inspiring account of overcoming hardship and a riveting adventure story as well.

Olaudah Equiano had important reasons for writing his autobiography. Many of those who traded or owned slaves had been made rich by slavery and were actively trying to defend it. They claimed that slaves were well-treated and happy. They said that Christianity permitted slavery and even endorsed it. They insisted that economic prosperity depended on slavery and it should never be abolished. They said that black people were strong but stupid, and so slavery suited them. They said that black people could never learn to read, much less to write a book.

Olaudah Equiano wanted to expose these claims as lies. Many people who were working to abolish slavery encouraged him to tell his story and helped him print his book. Olaudah wrote of his life not only for himself but for the millions of blacks still in slavery who could not make their voices heard. He knew that all Africans would be judged on the basis of his words. If he proved himself honest and intelligent, other black people might be seen that way, too. If he showed that he could write as powerfully as any white person, he would win respect both for himself and for other Africans suffering in bondage.

Olaudah Equiano knew how to tell a good story, and *The Interesting Narrative of the Life of Olaudah Equiano* became a bestseller soon after its publication in 1789. Within three years, eight editions were published in England and one in America. It became a classic and one of the founding works of a new branch of world literature: books written by Africans or people of African descent, captured or born into slavery and fighting to be free.

Olaudah's story portrayed both the graphic horrors of slavery and the boundless joys of freedom. And through his own example, he showed that a black person could be true to himself and still survive in a world he wanted no part of—and even make that world a better place. He showed that it was possible to use the tools of a cruel system—specifically, the printed word—to prompt change. His unwavering faith and insatiable desire for education served as beacons for other blacks. Even as a boy, Olaudah Equiano seems to have known that learning would give him power and control over his life. He learned how to box and how to cut hair; how to navigate a ship, how to ride a horse, and how to load a gun; how to do accounts and how to trade in order to buy his freedom. And, most important, he learned to read and write.

> I had often seen my master and Dick employed
> in reading; and I had a great curiosity to talk to
> the books, as I thought they did; and so to learn
> how all things had a beginning. For that purpose
> I have often taken up a book, and talked to it,
> and then put my ears to it, when alone, in hopes
> it would answer me; and I have been very much
> concerned when I found it remaining silent.

Once literate, Olaudah *could* make the book talk. For him and many others, this was an essential milestone; as the writer Ishmael Reed pointed out, the slave who learned to read and write was often the first to run away. Olaudah used his command of language not only to express his deepest feelings but also to affect the hearts and minds of thousands of readers. His words may even have changed the course of history.

Olaudah Equiano introduced in Western letters the inextricable link between literacy and freedom, between mastery of the written word and mastery of the self. By telling or writing the stories of their lives, more than 6,000 men and women contributed to the tradition of the "slave narrative"—the tradition that Equiano created. Many of them had read Equiano's book and used it as a guide. Directly and indirectly, his autobiography influenced the writing and thinking of such later African-American writers as Frederick Douglass, Booker T. Washington, Zora Neale Hurston, Martin Luther King, Jr., Malcolm X, and Maya Angelou.

It has been more than 200 years since Olaudah published his book. No one reads the writings of the long-dead slave owners and traders anymore. But Olaudah Equiano's autobiography is still in print and in bookstores, and every year it finds a new audience around the world. Ann Cameron's skillful adaptation helps make this great work accessible to readers of all ages. It is a compelling story of innocence betrayed and wisdom earned, of a human being's passage from freedom to slavery and back again. Through his words, Olaudah Equiano's indomitable spirit lives on.

—Henry Louis Gates, Jr.

About This Adaptation

When I read *The Interesting Narrative of the Life of Olaudah Equiano*, I thought it was a story children would love and should read. The original work is direct and active and exciting. But it is also an eighteenth-century book, written in the style of its time. It uses some words and conventional expressions we no longer use today. It is written in extremely long sentences, and with many incidental details of people and places. In Olaudah Equiano's time these details must have been very important evidence to prove to readers that he was a real person and that his story was true. To us today, they are not of so much interest.

In adapting the book, I modernized some of its language and shortened it. To me, the climactic moment of the story comes when Olaudah gains his freedom—the day he calls "the happiest day I had ever experienced." I ended this adaptation not long after that point—two-thirds of the way through the original narrative.

I wanted to provide a text that children could easily understand but also one that retained the flavor of the author's time, and, very often, his original language. Most of all, I wanted to be entirely faithful to the adventures, meanings, and spirit of Olaudah Equiano. I did not add any ideas of my own to his story or fictionalize it in any way.

—Ann Cameron

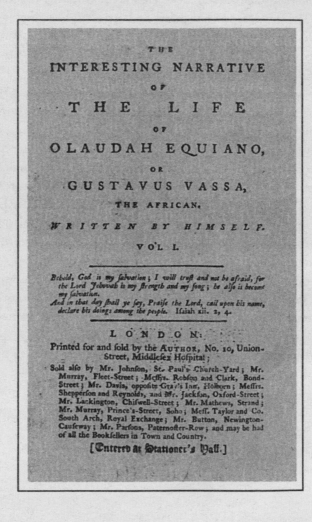

THE

INTERESTING NARRATIVE

OF

THE LIFE

OF

OLAUDAH EQUIANO,

OR

GUSTAVUS VASSA,

THE AFRICAN.

WRITTEN BY HIMSELF.

VOL I.

Behold, God is my salvation; I will trust and not be afraid, for the Lord Jehovah is my strength and my song; he also is become my salvation.
And in that day shall ye say, Praise the Lord, call upon his name, declare his doings among the people. Isaiah xii. 2, 4.

LONDON:

Printed for and sold by the AUTHOR, No. 10, Union-Street, Middlesex Hospital;

Sold also by Mr. Johnson, St. Paul's Church-Yard; Mr. Murray, Fleet-Street; Meſſrs. Robſon and Clark, Bond-Street; Mr. Davis, oppoſite Gray's Inn, Holborn; Meſſrs. Shepperſon and Reynolds, and Mr. Jackſon, Oxford-Street; Mr. Lackington, Chiſwell-Street; Mr. Mathews, Strand; Mr. Murray, Prince's-Street, Soho; Meſſ. Taylor and Co. South Arch, Royal Exchange; Mr. Button, Newington-Cauſeway; Mr. Parſons, Paternoſter-Row; and may be had of all the Bookſellers in Town and Country.

[Entered at Stationer's Hall.]

PROLOGUE

It is dangerous to publish the story of one's life. People who do are often accused of being vain. If unusual things have happened to them, they are rarely if ever believed. But if their story is too ordinary and too obvious, readers turn away in disgust.

Almost every experience in my life has made an impression on my mind, and influenced the way I act.

Some events in my life have happened to very few people. Others may not seem important.

But what makes any event important? I think no event is really important unless we use it to become better and wiser. To people who think about their lives, almost everything that happens, or that they read, provides a way of learning. To those who don't examine their lives, all the experience of the ages is worthless.

If I were a European, I would say I had suffered a lot. But I am an African. Compared to many of my people, I have suffered very little, and I consider myself a particular favorite of Heaven.

I didn't write my memoirs because I am vain, or to gain immortality or fame. I wrote them for my friends, who thought the world should know my story, and to serve the interests of humanity.

MY HOME

I was born not far from the Equator, in an African village. Our village was in the province of Essaka, in the kingdom of Benin.

Hundreds of miles to the south of us was the Guinea Coast, the ports where the slave traders came, and the shores of the Atlantic Ocean.

I was a child. I had never seen the ocean. I had never even heard of white men, or Europeans, or the sea.

Our town was far inland, in a beautiful fertile valley. Among us, nobody was a beggar and nobody was homeless. We were all farmers and warriors, and all of us, even the most important people, worked.

A few miles outside town, we cultivated fields

where we grew our food—bananas and yams, peppers and corn, and pineapples and many other fruits. We tapped small holes in palm trees and fastened empty gourds to them to collect delicious sweet palm wine. We raised cattle and goats and poultry too—to eat, but also to trade. We also traded a salt we made from ashes, and a kind of fragrant powdered earth. When this earth was thrown into a fire, it gave off a powerful sweet smell, like incense.

Men and women wore a perfume made of palm oil and a powdered, deliciously fragrant wood. Nobody drank alcohol—our palm wine had hardly any alcohol in it. Our people did smoke clay pipes—pipes with wooden stems so long that it took one or sometimes two boys to carry them.

Our women were alert, and modest and graceful, and on their legs and arms they wore many bracelets made of gold. Besides working in the fields with the men, they made pottery and spun and wove cotton. They used a berry to dye the cotton a beautiful shade of blue. Everybody, men and women and children, dressed in this blue cloth. Later on in my life I went to many places, but I never saw that special shade of blue.

Our people believed in a god—one Creator of all things, who lived in the sun. He didn't eat or drink, we thought, because of a belt that he wore tight around his waist. But sometimes, like us, he smoked a pipe.

We believed God controlled everything that happened. Especially, we thought, he decided things about our death, or our capture in battle. Also we believed that our dear friends and relations who had died watched over us and guarded us from bad spirits and from our enemies.

We never fought with our fists, or cursed, as Europeans do. The worst expressions we ever used were "May you rot!" or "May you swell!" or "May a beast take you!"

We were very clean, and had many rituals of washing. Anyone who touched the dead had to wash and purify himself before he could enter a house, or touch any person or anything we ate.

We were very careful not to eat poisoned food. Whenever we bought food to eat, the seller had to kiss it all over to show that it was not poisoned. Even at home we sometimes kissed food this way, especially if food and drink were being presented to a stranger.

Every time before we ate, we washed our hands. Then we poured a little food or drink on the ground in a special place. That was the offering we made to the good spirits who watched over us.

Our people all loved music. Almost every person in our town was a poet, a musician, and a dancer. We celebrated every important event with big public dances, with songs and music made up just for that occasion. We played drums, and an instrument like a guitar, and one like a sticcado. Our songs were about the things that mattered to us. For that reason, they were always new and changing, and full of life.

Our biggest holiday was New Year's. On New Year's Day, when the sun set, we set up a cheer that could be heard all the way across our country, and we made a tremendous noise with rattles. Then we made many offerings to the spirits of our ancestors, and the children who were supposed to be lucky were carried around and shown to all the people. When I was small, I was carried around that way.

Some of our families had slaves. Our slaves were prisoners we had captured in battle, or people who had committed some crime. They worked just the same as we did, no more, and their food and clothing and houses were just the same as ours. Some of our slaves even had slaves under them, to help them. We treated them just the same as us, except for one thing: they were not permitted to eat at the same table with free people.

In town, each family had its own land, surrounded by moats and wooden fences or, sometimes, red-clay brick walls.

Every head of a family had one wife, or sometimes two. The wives were considered his property. He had one wooden house for himself and others for his wives and children and his slaves. Whenever someone needed a house, the whole village helped build it. The only thing people expected in return was a feast.

Because my father had many slaves, his piece of land was very big. It was like a little village in itself, full of one-story thatched-roof houses.

The floors of the houses were covered with reed mats. Our chairs were wooden logs. Our beds were wooden platforms three or four feet high. On top of them we laid the spongy parts of plantain trees; they made soft mattresses that we covered with animal skins.

Our town had bearded wise men, the ah-affoe-way-cah. They calculated our calendar and foretold events. They were our doctors too: they healed wounds and cured people who had been poisoned.

We respected them, but also we feared them. When an ah-affoe-way-cah died, only other wise men went to his funeral. The wise man who had died would be buried after sunset, with many of his tools and valuable things. Afterward, the other wise men would always return from his burial place a different way from the one they had taken to get there.

When I was born, the wise men told everyone I

would be lucky. I was named Olaudah, which in our language means "fortunate" and "someone who speaks well, with a loud voice."

We had many snakes, and some of them, we thought, gave us omens of the future. When I was small, two enormous snakes, thick as a man's leg, crept into my mother's house one night while we were sleeping.

We told the wise men the snakes were with us. The wise men said that I should touch them, because it would bring me luck. I put my hand on the snakes, which were harmless and very tame. Then we put them on a big earthenware pan and carried them out to the road.

Another time a poisonous snake crossed the road and passed between my feet without touching me. The people who saw this were very surprised. The wise men, and my mother and the rest of the people too, thought these were remarkable omens in my favor.

The villages of Benin were all independent of each other, and the king of Benin did not really control them. The only government I knew of was our village chiefs. The chiefs were called embrenches. They made rules and settled arguments and punished crimes. Being an embrenche was a big job—like being a prince, a judge, and a senator, all in one.

My father was an embrenche. Like all the embrenches, he had a special ceremonial mark. In a ritual, the skin on his forehead had been cut and rolled down to his eyebrows and then pressed against his head. His face bore the mark of the healed wound—a thick band of skin across his forehead. It was called the mark of greatness.

I had watched one of my older brothers go through the ritual to become an embrenche. One day I would become an embrenche too, and my parents would give me that mark.

KIDNAPPED!

In our village we were always ready for war. These wars were usually surprise attacks from strangers from another district who wanted to take prisoners or booty. Often, the attacks came when we were out of the village, working in the fields.

When we were afraid of the village being invaded, we guarded the streets leading to our houses with stakes struck into the ground. The exposed ends of the stakes had sharp points dipped in poison. The attacker who stepped on one would die.

It took a couple of hours to walk to our fields from the village. To prevent surprise attacks on the way to the fields, neighbors always walked together, carrying their hoes and axes and shovels—and their weapons too.

Our weapons were guns, bows and arrows, and broad two-edged swords. We also had spears, and also huge shields that could cover a man from head to foot.

Everybody was taught how to use these

weapons, even the women. Our whole district was like a volunteer army. We all knew the warning signals, like the firing of a gun at night. When a signal came, we grabbed our weapons and rushed out of our houses to fight.

Children were warriors too. From when I was very little I was trained to fight. Every day I practiced shooting and spear-throwing. My mother decorated me with the emblems of war, the same ones our greatest fighters used.

Once when I was small I saw a battle in the fields. We were all working there, when we were suddenly attacked. I climbed a tree at a distance and watched the fight. There were many women, as well as men, on both sides. I saw my mother fighting, swinging her broadsword.

A furious battle raged for a long time, and many people were killed. Then our village won and took the enemy's chief as prisoner.

We carried him back to the village in triumph. He offered a big ransom for his life, but we would not accept it. He was put to death. It was always the enemy chiefs who started the fighting. We knew any who went free would bring a new army and return to do us harm.

A young woman among our enemies had been slain in the battle. We hung her arm in the market, where we always showed the trophies of battle. The weapons and belongings of the enemy fighters were divided among the warriors. We awarded the most to those who had fought best. The prisoners who were not sold or ransomed we kept as slaves.

I had five older brothers and one sister. Because I was the youngest, I was my mother's favorite. I went everywhere with her.

Often when I went with her to market, we saw strangers—big men who carried huge empty sacks. We called them Oye-Ibo, which meant "red men living at a distance." They brought with them things we didn't have—firearms, gunpowder, hats, beads, and dried fish. They traded these things with us to get the things they didn't have—fragrant wood and earth, and the salt we made of wood ashes.

They always carried slaves with them too; but we didn't let them cross our land until they had explained how they got the slaves. Sometimes we sold slaves to them—but only prisoners of war, or our own people who had been convicted of kidnapping or other crimes.

I didn't know it then, but now I think that getting salt and fragrant woods was not the traders' real purpose. Probably slaves were what they wanted most. With offers of guns and gunpowder and other things from Europe, they tempted the rival chiefs into their desperate prisoner-taking raids.

When the grown people went to the fields to work, usually we children stayed behind in the village to play. Kidnappers would take advantage of our parents' being away to carry off as many of us as they could seize. Usually, some of us would get up in trees to be lookouts and watch for strangers.

One day, as I was watching at the top of a tree in our yard, I saw a kidnapper come into a neighbor's yard. There were lots of children playing there, and he intended to take some—but I gave the alarm.

The strongest children came running with ropes. They tangled him up in so many cords he had no way to get loose. We held him like that till some grown-ups came and took him prisoner.

But not long after, another attack came, and that day there were no grown-ups nearby.

I was eleven. I was with my only sister, who was always my favorite playmate. As usual, all the grown-ups were gone to the fields. My sister and I were left to take care of the house.

Two men and a woman got over our walls, and in a moment seized us both. We had no chance to cry out or resist. Quickly they covered our mouths and ran off with us into the woods.

They stopped to tie our hands. Then they carried us again, as far as they could, till night came on.

We reached a small house, where the robbers halted to eat and spend the night. They untied us and offered us food, but we couldn't eat, we were so choked with tiredness and grief. Finally sleep came. For a little while it took away our pain.

The next morning we left the house, and continued traveling all day. For a long time we stayed in the woods, but at last we came into a road which I believed I knew. I saw some people at a distance. As loud as I could, I cried for help. The kidnappers tied me tighter, stopped my mouth, and put me into an enormous sack. They gagged my sister too, and tied her hands; and so we went on till the people who might have helped us were out of sight.

The next night when we went to rest, the kidnappers offered us food again, but we refused it. All night we held each other and cried. But soon we lost even the small comfort of crying together. The next day the kidnappers pulled my sister away from me. We held on to each other and begged them not to separate us, but the kidnappers took my sister and carried her away.

I went almost crazy from losing her. I cried all the time. For several days I wouldn't eat anything except what the kidnappers forced into my mouth.

I PLAN TO RUN AWAY

We traveled many days, and I often changed masters. Finally, I got into the hands of a chieftain in a pleasant country. Although I was a great many days' journey from my father's house, these people spoke our language.

This man had two wives and some children. They treated me extremely well, and did all they could to comfort me, particularly the first wife, who was something like my mother. Still, I was weighed down by homesickness for my mother and my friends. Also, I didn't dare to eat with the freeborn children, even though I mostly was with them. That made me want my freedom even more.

My new master was a goldsmith. I pumped air on his fire from a bellows made of leather, so he could make gold ornaments.

After I had been in this place about a month, they all started to trust me a little way from the house. I used my freedom to ask the way to my own home.

I sometimes went with the older girls in the cool of the evenings to bring pitchers of water home from the springs. I found opportunities to ask my way then too.

Every day during my journey I had watched where the sun rose in the morning and set in the evening. I knew that my father's house was toward the east. I planned to seize the first chance to escape, and to go in the direction of the rising sun.

But while I was planning my escape, I had an unlucky accident.

I used to help an elderly woman slave cook and take care of the poultry. One morning, while I was feeding some chickens, I threw a stone at one of them. The stone hit it right in its middle and killed it.

The old slave woman soon missed the chicken and asked me where it was. My mother had taught me not to lie. I told the old woman my stone had killed it.

She flew into a rage. "You'll suffer for that!" she said. Right away she went to tell her mistress what I had done.

This scared me very much. I expected an

instant flogging, and I dreaded it. I had almost never been beaten at home.

I decided to escape. I ran into a thicket nearby, and hid in the bushes. Soon afterward my mistress and the slave returned. They didn't see me, but I could see them, searching the whole house and all around, calling for me.

I didn't answer.

They thought I had run away, and they alerted everyone in the neighborhood to pursue me.

In that part of the country, and where my family had lived too, the woods were so thick that a person could hide and escape the closest search. The neighbors looked for me the whole day. Several times many of them came within a few yards of the place where I lay hid. When I heard a rustling in the trees, I expected them to find me any minute and take me back to be punished by my master. But they never found me.

They were often so near that I even heard them guess where I might be. "He's trying to get home," someone said, "but it's so far and such a hard trip that he'll never make it." When I heard that I felt a terrible panic. I despaired.

Night came on, and increased my fears. I had planned to start home at dark, but the searchers had convinced me it was useless. Even if I could escape all the other animals, I was afraid I couldn't escape the human ones. Even if I did escape them, I didn't know the way. I could end up dying in the woods.

I heard rustlings in the leaves. It was probably snakes moving in the dark. Any second, one could bite me. I left the thicket. I crept to my master's kitchen, which was an open shed, and laid myself down in the ashes, wishing for death. I was barely awake in the morning when the old woman slave, who was first up, came to light the fire, and saw me in the fireplace. She was so surprised to see me, she could hardly believe her eyes. She went to the master, and asked him to be kind to me.

He soon came. He scolded me a little, but he ordered me to be taken care of and not ill treated.

Soon after this my master's only child by his first wife got sick and died. He felt very bad. For some time he was almost frantic. He really would have killed himself, but people watched him all the time and kept him from doing it.

Soon afterward he recovered, and I was sold again.

I MEET MY SISTER

I was carried to the left of the sun's rising, through dismal woods where wild beasts roared. The people I was sold to were well armed, but they were not unkind. When I was tired they used to carry me, either on their shoulders or on their backs. At night we slept in well-built houses along the side of road. Merchants and regular travelers had built these houses for shelter.

We traveled like this a long time, so long that I learned two or three new languages in order to speak to people.

One night in the house where we were sheltered, a girl was brought in—my own dear sister! As soon as she saw me, she screamed and ran into my arms. For a long time all we could do was cling to each other and cry.

When the people knew we were brother and sister, they let us be together. The man to whom we belonged slept between us, and all night she and I held each other's hands across his sleeping body. Until morning we forgot all our troubles in the joy of being together. But as soon as the sun had risen, our owner sold my sister. She was torn away from me, and all my misery returned.

What would happen to us? I didn't know. But I was afraid she was going to suffer even more than me—and I would not be there to help her.

I loved her very much. I would have stood every pain for her. I would have won freedom for her, even if it meant I never got my own. Much later, when things went well for me, I would think of her and become sad. When things were bad for me, I would think of her and feel even more bitter.

We had spent our last night together. I would never forget her. I never saw her again.

TINNAH,
THE SCARRED PEOPLE

I too was soon sold, and traveled on till after a long time I came to a town called Tinnah, in the most beautiful country I had ever seen in Africa. The town had many streams, and a pond in the center of town where people washed. They had coconuts, and sugarcane, which I had never tasted before. For money the people used little white sea shells, the size of a fingernail.

A wealthy widow bought me for 172 of these seashells. She wanted me for a companion for her only son. She took me to her house and I was washed, and ate with him and became his play-mate. The language his people spoke was so much like mine that I understood him perfectly. I was older than my new friend, and he always treated me with respect. He would never start to eat until I had started.

Slaves waited on us, and we played with darts and bows and arrows, the way I used to do at home. For two months I lived like this. I started to feel happy and forget the terrible things that had happened to me. I thought I was going to be adopted into the family.

But one morning early, while her son was still asleep, the widow woke me up and hurried me away, to sell me.

Now I was carried off among people who used iron pots for cooking and had European crossbows and cutlasses for weapons—things I had never seen before. What most amazed me was that they didn't make any offerings to God or the spirits of their ancestors.

These people ate without washing their hands and fought with their fists. They ornamented themselves with scars and filed their teeth to sharp points. They wanted to scar me too, and file my teeth, but I wouldn't let them do it.

At last we came to the banks of a large river. I had never seen any body of water larger than a pond, and the size of the river amazed me.

Here by the river, the people didn't live in houses at all—they lived in big canoes where they kept everything they owned. At times people dived from the canoes and swam. Both men and women did it. I was amazed again. In our village we didn't know how to swim.

Soon I was put into one of the canoes. We began to paddle and move along the river. I was very surprised—and afraid.

We continued till evening, when we came to land. Some families dragged their canoes on shore and made fires on the riverbank. Others cooked in their canoes and slept in them all night. The canoe I was in was beached. Reed mats were used to make tents in the shape of little houses, and inside them we slept.

THE SLAVE SHIP

So I traveled both by land and by water, through different countries, till, six or seven months after I had been kidnapped, I arrived at the coast.

The first thing I saw was a vast ocean, and a ship, riding at anchor, waiting for its cargo. The ocean and the ship filled me with astonishment that soon turned to fear. I was taken to the ship and carried on board!

The crew had strange complexions and long hair. Their language was very different from any I had ever heard. Some of them thumped me and tossed me around to see if I was healthy. I was sure that I had got into a world of bad spirits and that they were going to kill me.

I was terrified. I wished I was anyone but me. I would rather have been even the lowest slave in my own country. If I had owned ten thousand worlds, I would have given them all to change my lot for his.

When I looked round the ship I saw a furnace

boiling on the deck, and many black people all chained together, every one of their faces full of sorrow. I was overpowered by horror, and fainted. When I recovered, I saw some black people around me. They were some of those who had brought me on board, and they were receiving their pay. They tried to cheer me, but in vain.

I asked them if we were not to be eaten by those white men with horrible looks, red faces, and long hair.

"No," they said.

A white man brought me a little liquor in a wineglass. I was afraid of him, and wouldn't take it out of his hand. A black took it from him and gave it to me, and I swallowed a little of it. I never had had alcohol before. The strange sensation it gave me threw me into the greatest consternation.

Soon after this the blacks who had brought me on board went off the ship, and left me abandoned to despair. I had no chance now of returning to my country—and not even the smallest chance of getting back to shore.

The crew took me down below decks, into the ship's stinking hold. With the horribleness of the stench and my crying I was so sick and low that I couldn't eat. I wanted to die.

Two white men offered me food, but I refused to eat. Then one of them held me fast by the hands and laid me across the windlass. He tied my feet, while the other flogged me.

When they let me loose I wanted to jump into the sea. Even though I couldn't swim and I was afraid of the water, I still wanted to do it. I couldn't. Nets were stretched all along the sides of the ship, and they were too high for me to jump. Besides, the sailors watched us all the time if we weren't chained down to the decks.

Days later, I saw some poor Africans severely whipped for trying to jump overboard. And every hour there were Africans whipped for not eating. It often happened to me.

That first day, among the poor chained men in the hold, I found some people of Benin.

"What are they going to do to us?" I asked.

"They are taking us away to work for them," a man from Benin explained.

"And do they only live here," I asked, "in this hollow place, the ship?"

"They have a white people's country," the man explained, "but it is far away."

"How can it be," I asked, "that in our whole country nobody ever heard of them?"

"They live *very* far away," another man explained.

"Where are their women?" I asked. "Do they have any?"

"Yes," the first man said.

"And why don't we see them?"

"They leave them behind."

"How can the ship go?" I asked.

"We don't know exactly," they said. "They put cloth on those tall poles with the help of ropes. Then the vessel goes. Besides that, they have some spell or magic they put in the water to make the ship stop when they want it to."

I was exceedingly amazed at this account and really thought the white people were spirits from another world. I really wanted to get away from them. But I felt a little less scared, knowing they were taking us to work. If that was all they did to me, I could stand it.

Despite what the men from Benin told me, I was often afraid I should be put to death, the white people looked and acted so savage. I had never seen such brutal cruelty.

At times while we were anchored off the coast I and many others were permitted to stay on deck. One day, to my great astonishment, I saw one of the ships coming in with its sails up. As soon as the whites saw it, they gave a great shout, at which we were amazed. The vessel got larger as it got nearer, and then the anchor was let go. I and my countrymen were convinced it was done by magic.

Soon after this the other ship got her boats out,

and they came on board of us.* The people of both ships seemed very glad to see each other. Several of the strangers shook hands with us black people, and made signs with their hands. I suppose they were trying to tell us that we were going to their country, but we did not understand them.

At last our ship got in all her cargo. The crew made the ship ready with many frightening noises. We were all put under deck, so that we could not see how they managed the vessel.

In the hold of the ship many of us died, victims of the greed of our purchasers. All of us were penned up together, crowded so close that we could hardly turn around. Our chains galled us. Open tubs were used for toilets. Often children fell into them and nearly drowned. The heat caused heavy perspiration, and the air became unfit to breathe. It sickened us. It almost suffocated us. And in this thick, fetid, pestilential air the shrieks of women and the groans of the dying vibrated hour upon hour.

Fortunately, I was soon so near death that they kept me on the deck almost all the time, and because I was so young, I wasn't chained. Nearly every day some of my companions were brought

*Small boats were stored on the ship to use in case of shipwreck, and to carry people and supplies from ship to shore and from one ship to another.

upon deck at the point of death. I hoped that I would soon die too. Often I thought that the inhabitants of the deep were much happier than I. I envied the fish their freedom, and I wished I could have changed my lot for theirs.

Everything I saw convinced me more of the cruelty of the whites. One day they netted a lot of fish. They killed and ate all they wanted. Those of us who were on the deck begged for some fish, but they threw the rest back into the sea. A few of my countrymen who were very hungry tried to take some fish when they thought no one was watching, but they were caught, and flogged severely. And the cruelty wasn't only toward us blacks, but also toward some of the whites themselves. Once I saw a white man flogged so unmercifully with a rope that he died; and they tossed him over the side of the ship like a dead animal.

During our trip I saw flying fish, which surprised me very much. They used to fly across the ship, and many of them fell on the deck. Also I saw the first use of the ship's quadrant. I had often seen the sailors make observations with it. One of them let me look through it. The moving clouds looked to me like land that disappeared. But how could land disappear! I was sure that I was in another world, and everything around me was magic.

Barbados.
The Auction

One day the whites on board gave a great shout, and made many signs of joy to us. We did not know why, but as the vessel drew nearer we plainly saw the island of Barbados and its harbor, and other ships of different kinds and sizes. Soon we anchored among them off Bridgetown.

Many merchants and planters came on board, though it was in the evening. They put us in separate groups, and examined us, and made us jump. They pointed to the land, signifying we were to go there. We thought these ugly men meant they were going to beat us soon. Then we were all put down under the deck again.

There was much dread and trembling among us, and nothing but bitter cries to be heard all night. At last the crew, who heard us, got some old slaves from the land to calm us. They told us no one was going to eat us. We were going to work. Soon we would go on land, and see many of our countrypeople. This report relieved us, and we could sleep. And, sure enough, not long after we landed, Africans of all languages came to talk to us.

Right away we were taken to a merchant's yard, where we were all penned up together like so many sheep. When I looked out at the town, everything was new to me. The houses were built with bricks, in stories, and were completely different from any I had seen in Africa. I was still more astonished at seeing people on horseback. I thought it was more magic, but one of the slaves with me said that the horses were the same kind they had in his country.

We were not many days in the merchant's custody before we were sold—like this:

Someone beat a drum. Then all the buyers rushed at once into the yard where we were penned to choose the parcel of us that they liked best. They rushed from one group of us to another, with tremendous noise and eager faces, terrifying us all.

Three men who were sold were brothers. They were sold in different lots. I still remember how they cried when they were parted. Probably they never saw each other again.

I didn't know it, but this happened all the time in slave sales. Parents lost their children; brothers lost their sisters. Husbands lost their wives.

We had already lost our homes, our countries, and almost everyone we loved. The people who did the selling and buying could have done it without separating us from our very last relatives and friends. They already could live in riches from our misery and toil. What possible advantage did they gain from this refinement of cruelty? But they practiced it—and went to church on Sunday, and said that they were Christian.

To Virginia

Now I had no comfort talking to people from home. All my countrymen had been sold. The kind women, who used to wash me and take care of me, were also all gone different ways, and I never saw one of them afterward.

After the sale, I and a few others were left in the merchant's yard. Because we had fretted in captivity so much, we were sick and weak. No one would buy us.

In a few days the merchant put us on a ship again—a sloop bound for North America. We were better treated on this trip than coming up from Africa, and they fed us plenty of rice and fat pork.

We landed in the colony of Virginia, up a river a good way from the sea, about Virginia County. We saw very few Africans, and not one soul who could talk to me.

For a few weeks I weeded grass and gathered stones on a plantation. At last all my companions were distributed different ways. I was the only one left. I was now exceedingly lonesome and miserable—worse off than any of the rest of my companions. They could talk to each other. I could not talk to a single person who understood what I said. I was constantly grieving and pining, and wishing for death.

While I was on this plantation, the owner of it got sick, and I was sent to his house. When I walked into the house, I saw a black woman slave, who was cooking the dinner. She was working cruelly loaded down with strange iron devices. The worst was one on her head. It locked her mouth so tight that she could scarcely speak, and could not eat or drink. Later I found out this horrible thing was called an "iron muzzle."

Full of fear, I kept on my way through the house. I came into the room where the plantation owner was. A fan was put into my hand, to fan the gentleman while he slept.

While he was fast asleep, I looked around the room, which to me was very fine and strange. The first thing I noticed was a clock that hung on the chimney and was moving. I was quite surprised at the noise it made, and I was afraid it would tell the gentleman anything I might do wrong.

Then I saw a portrait hanging in the room. It seemed to be looking at me all the time. I got still more frightened. I had never seen such a thing before.

At first I thought it was something related to magic. Then, when it didn't move, I thought it might be some way the whites had to preserve their great men when they died. Maybe, I thought, they offer their friendly spirits food, the way we do in Benin. But this thought didn't make me any less scared of the picture. I stayed frightened till my master awoke. He dismissed me from the room—to my great satisfaction and relief, for I thought that these people were all made up of wonders.

SAVED!

I had been miserable, forlorn, and dejected for some time when the kind and unknown hand of God reached out to comfort me.

A sea captain came to my master's house on business. His name was Michael Henry Pascal. Captain Pascal was a lieutenant in the Royal Navy, but he was commanding a trading ship, the *Industrious Bee*. While he was at my master's house he saw me, and liked me so well that he purchased me. He thought of giving me as a present to some of his friends in England. I think he paid thirty or forty pounds sterling for me.

After the sale I was guided by an elderly black man and sent to the ship on horseback—a way of traveling that was very strange to me. Then I was carried on board a fine large ship, loaded with tobacco, just ready to sail for England.

Everybody on board was very kind to me—not like any white people I had seen before. The crew gave me sails to lie on, and plenty of good food. I started to think white people were not all the same.

A few days after I was on board, we sailed to England. I had no idea where I was going, or why. But by this time I could talk a little English.

"Where are we going?" I asked.

"We're going to carry you back to your own country," some of the people on the ship told me. This made me very happy. I rejoiced to hear we were going back to Africa. What wonders I would tell my family! But when we saw the English coast, I was undeceived.

On board an earlier ship I had been called Michael, but on the plantation they had called me Jacob. Now on board the *Industrious Bee*, Captain Pascal named me Gustavus Vassa.

I understood him a little and told him I didn't like that name.

"I want to be called Jacob," I said.

He said no, and still called me Gustavus.

At first I refused to answer to my new name, but he cuffed me for it. Finally I gave up. I have been known as Gustavus Vassa ever since.

The ship had a very long passage, and we ran short of food.

"We are going to kill and eat you," the captain and the crew told me.

They were joking, but I thought they were serious and got very depressed. While I was worrying about it, they caught a big shark and pulled it on board. I was very happy. They could eat it instead of me!

But they only cut a small piece off the tail. When they threw the rest of the shark over the side, all my worries came back to me.

There was a boy named Dick on board the ship, who was about four or five years older than me. He had never been at sea before. His full name was Richard Baker, and he was an American. He had received an excellent education and was very friendly. We became inseparable, and for the next two years he was my friend and teacher. His family owned many slaves, but he had a mind above prejudice. He was not afraid to be the friend of someone who was ignorant, a stranger, and a slave.

My master, Captain Pascal, had lodged in Dick's mother's house in America and respected him very much. He always made Dick eat with him in the cabin.

He used to joke with Dick and say, "I'm going to kill Gustavus and eat him!"

He asked me, "Are black people good to eat? Don't you eat people in your country?"

I said "No!"

He said, "Then I'll kill Dick first, and you afterward."

I got a little less worried about myself, but I was very alarmed for Dick. Whenever the captain called him, I would peep and watch to see if they were going to kill him. I got free from this worry only when we reached land.

One night we lost a man overboard. There was great noise and confusion, and cries of "Stop the ship!" I didn't know what was the matter, and got very scared.

The waves were very high. I thought the Ruler of the seas was angry. Perhaps to appease him the crew would perform some magic—and sacrifice me.

My mind was filled with agony. All night I couldn't close my eyes. When daylight appeared, I was a little less scared, but still, when I was called, I was afraid I might be killed.

Some time after this, right at dusk we saw some very large fish. Afterward I found out they were called grampuses. They looked to me extremely terrible. They were so near they blew water on the ship's deck. I thought *they* were the rulers of the sea. But the white people did not make any offerings.

I thought, "The fish must be angry!"

The wind died away, and the ship stopped moving.

I thought, "The fish must have stopped our ship! Soon, the crew will appease the fish by making an offering of me!"

I ran and hid in the fore part of the ship.

I trembled in my hiding place and kept peeking out sometimes to see what was going on. My good friend Dick missed me. He started searching for me and soon found me. I asked him about the fish.

I still didn't speak much English. I could hardly make him understand my question. He didn't understand at all when I asked about offerings.

"Those fish will devour anybody!" Dick said. That answer didn't calm me.

Then Captain Pascal, who was leaning over the quarterdeck railing and looking at the fish, called Dick.

Dick told the captain about my fears, so the captain called me to him and entertained everybody with my fears and crying and trembling.

All the while, the crew was setting fire to a barrel of pitch to give the fish to play with. Finally they got it lighted and put it over the side of the ship into the water.

It was just dark. The flaming barrel floated away from us, and the fish went after it. To my great joy, I saw them no more.

ENGLAND

After thirteen weeks we reached the coast of England. All my alarms about being eaten began to subside.

Sure enough, as soon as the ship reached Falmouth, the captain went on shore and sent fresh provisions on board. We made good use of them, and our famine turned to feasting.

Almost every day, something new surprised me.

One morning when I got up on deck, I saw it all covered over with white stuff. I ran down to the mate and told him, as well as I could, to come and see how somebody in the night had thrown salt all over the deck.

"Bring some of it down to me," he said.

I gathered a handful—it was very cold—and brought it to him.

"Taste it," he said.

I did, and I was amazed.

"It's snow," he said, but I couldn't understand him.

He asked me if we had snow in my country, and I said no.

I asked him who made it.

"A great man in the heavens, called God," he said, but here again I couldn't understand him.

After this I went on land in Falmouth. I was amazed at the paved streets and the brick buildings. We went to church, and I was amazed at the service. I asked all I could about it, and they told me it was "worshipping God, who made us and all things." I still couldn't understand anything, but my friend Dick tried to explain it to me.

I liked the idea of this God. I liked it that the white people didn't sell each other, as we Africans did. I thought that made them happier than us.

I was astonished at the wisdom of the white people in all the things I saw. But I was amazed at their not sacrificing, or making offerings, and their eating with unwashed hands, and touching the dead. Also I noticed the slenderness of the white women, which I did not like at first. I didn't think they were as pretty as our African women.

It was very strange to me to see my master and Dick reading. I had a great curiosity to talk to the books, as I thought they did. The books, I thought, would tell me how all things had a beginning.

When nobody was around, I would pick up a book, and talk to it, and then put my ear to it. I hoped that it would answer me. I was very disappointed and surprised when it remained silent.

It was near the beginning of spring 1757 when I arrived in England. I was nearly twelve years old.

My master lodged at the house of a gentleman in Falmouth. He had a little daughter about six or seven years old. She liked me very much, so much that we ate together and had servants to wait on us. I was so well treated by this family that it often reminded me of my little African master, whose mother had bought me for 172 shells.

After I had been in Falmouth a few days, I was sent on board the ship. But the little girl cried because she missed me. Nothing could calm her till I was sent for again.

But I was scared when I went back to her house! I didn't know anything about English customs. It seems ridiculous now, but I was terribly worried that they would make me engaged to marry this young lady. And when my master asked me if I would stay there with her behind him, as he was going away with the ship, which had been loaded with a cargo of tobacco, I cried immediately and said I would not leave him. So one night he took me from the house by stealth and brought me back on board the ship again.

We sailed to the island of Guernsey, where my master placed me to board and lodge with one of his mates, who had a wife and family there. My friend Dick stayed with us too.

This mate had a little daughter, Mary, about five or six years old. Her mother was very kind to me. She taught me everything just the way she did her own child, and in every way she treated me just like her own child.

She used to wash Mary's face, and mine. When she washed Mary's face, it looked rosy; but when she washed mine, it didn't. I tried to see if I could make my face the same color as Mary's by washing it. But it was all in vain. I started to be embarrassed at the difference in our complexions.

I stayed with this family until the summer of 1757. Then a great change came in my life. My master left his trading ship, and returned to service in the navy. He was appointed first lieutenant of his majesty's ship the *Roebuck*. He sent for Dick and me, and his old mate. Right away we all left Guernsey, and set out for England to join the ship and the war against France.★

★ In America this war was called "The French and Indian War." It was a fight between England and France about who should control Canada. The French, who were supported by their Indian allies, wanted Canada so they could make money from the fur trade. The English wanted it as a place where English people could live and farm.

THE PRESS GANG

We were on a sloop bound for London. As we were coming up toward the river Nore, where the *Roebuck* lay, a man-of-war's boat came alongside.

"They're going to press us!" someone shouted.

Each and every man ran to hide.

I didn't know what was happening, or what to think, but I ran too and hid under a hen coop.

The press gang came on board with their swords drawn. They searched and pulled men out by force, and put them into the boat.

At last they found me too. The man who discovered me held me up by the heels, while they all teased me. I screamed and cried the whole time as loud as I could. Finally, the mate came to help me. He told me they wouldn't take me, but I only felt safe when the man-of-war's boat pulled away.*

Soon afterward we reached the *Roebuck*. To my great joy, my master came on board to us, and brought us to the ship.

---

* When a warship was short of hands, the captain sent out crew members to kidnap sailors from other ships or from the shore. The kidnappers were called a press gang. The men the press gang took away might have had to sail on the man-of-war for as long as three years, unless they landed somewhere where they could escape. Not enough men wanted to sail on warships, so England allowed the kidnapping so it could win wars. Being an impressed sailor was a kind of slavery—but the sailor couldn't be bought or sold, eventually got free, and got paid for his work.

To War

The *Roebuck* was a huge ship filled with men and guns, but I wasn't afraid the way I was when I first saw Europeans. The more I learned, the less I was surprised by them. Instead of being scared, for a while I went to the opposite extreme. I was fearless. I even began to long for a battle.

There were a lot of boys my age on board the *Roebuck*. We were always together, and we spent a lot of our time playing. My griefs wore away, and I starting enjoying myself. I had suffered a lot, but I was too young to be sad all the time.

One day, we boys were called on the quarter-deck and made to fight each other. The sailors placed bets on who would win. This was the first time I ever fought with a white boy. He gave me a bloody nose, which I had never had before. This made me fight desperately, I think more than an hour, until we both were tired and the crew separated us.

The *Roebuck* sailed to many places. We went to
Holland twice. Later we went to Scotland, and
from there to the Orkney Islands, where there was
hardly any night. We chased some French ships off
the coast of France and took them captive without
a fight. I learned many of the maneuvers of the
ship, and several times I fired the guns.

When we got back to England, Dick and I and
my master stayed with his cousins in London—Mr.
Guerin and his two sisters, the Miss Guerins. These
two sisters were very good to me.

I wanted to see everything in London—but
from the winter cold and the damp, my feet got
inflamed and infected. For several months I
couldn't even stand up. Captain Pascal sent me to
the hospital St. George, where I got even sicker.
My leg was infected, and several times the doctors
wanted to cut it off. They were afraid the infection
would spread and kill me.

But I wouldn't let them cut my leg off. I told
them I would rather die than lose it. Thank God, I
recovered without an operation. Then just when
I was ready to leave the hospital, I got smallpox. I
felt very unlucky, but I soon got better, and went
to join my master and Dick on another ship, a
fifty-gun man-of-war, the *Preston*.

Very soon, my master was promoted to lieutenant of a very big ship, the *Royal George*. Dick

was going to stay on the *Preston* and sail to Turkey. I had to decide whether to stay with Dick, or change ships with my master.

My master wanted me to stay on the *Preston*, where I could learn to play the French horn, but I told him that if he left me behind, it would break my heart.

Finally he agreed to take me with him.

Soon Dick and I hugged each other and said our good-byes. We didn't know it was for the last time.

The *Royal George* was the largest ship I'd ever seen, with large brass guns. While we were in port, there were men, women and children on it, and shops and stalls for every kind of goods, and people shouting out their wares around—just like the ship was a town. To me it seemed like a little world— where once again I had no friend, because I had left my dear companion, Dick.

Soon we made another change. The whole crew of the *Royal George* transferred to the *Namur*, the ship of Vice Admiral Boscawen. My master was promoted to be sixth lieutenant on the *Namur*, which soon joined an enormous fleet of men-of-war headed for Canada.

Contrary winds blew the whole fleet off-course. Instead of getting to America, we were driven to the island of Teneriffe, off the northwest coast of

Africa. But when the weather changed, we set off again. It wasn't long before we got into harbor in Canada at St. George, in Halifax, where we had lots of fish to eat, and fresh provisions.

Other men-of-war joined us, and transport ships with soldiers. When our fleet had grown to an enormous size, we all sailed to Cape Breton.

The head of all the English land forces, General Wolfe, was on board our ship. He was friendly to all the men, and they loved him. He often paid attention to me and other boys too. Once I was supposed to be flogged for fighting with a young gentleman, but General Wolfe saved me from punishment.

We got to Cape Breton in the summer of 1758, where we had to land the English soldiers to attack the French town of Louisbourg.

My master was one of the lieutenants who superintended the landing. The French knew we were coming and they were ready for us, dug into trenches on the shore. Just as one of our lieutenants gave a word of command, a French musket ball went through his open mouth and came out his cheek.

Many soldiers were killed on both sides. The French fought us for a long time, but at last they were driven from their positions. All our soldiers landed and chased them as far as Louisbourg.

That day I held in my hand the scalp of an Indian king killed in the battle. He had been fighting on the side of the French. A Scottish Highlander had taken his scalp. I saw the king's ornaments too. They were very curious, and made of feathers.

Our land forces laid siege to Louisbourg. The French men-of-war were blocked up in the harbor by our fleet, and batteries of our guns fired on them from the land. Some French ships were set on fire by the shells from the batteries, and three of them burned up completely.

About fifty boats belonging to the English men-of-war attacked the only two remaining French men-of-war in the harbor. They set fire to a seventy-gun ship, and captured one with sixty-four guns.

At last Louisbourg was taken. The English men-of-war came into the harbor, and we had the most beautiful procession on the water I had ever seen. Our ships were decorated with all kinds of colors, from the top gallant masthead to the deck. All the admirals and captains were in full-dress uniform, and their barges were decorated with pennants.

Vice Admiral Boscawen went on shore in his

barge, followed by the other officers in order of seniority, and they took possession of the fort and the town. Sometime after this the French governor, his lady, and other important people came on board our ship to dine.

After the battle, and the celebration, I had a lot of free time, and I often went on shore in Louisbourg. As soon as everything was settled, we sailed with Admiral Boscawen and part of the fleet to England.

It was the winter of 1758 when we neared the English coast. One evening at dusk we were looking for land, when we saw seven large men-of-war standing offshore. Within forty minutes we got close enough to hail them.

"They're English," several people said; and they even began to name the ships.

In a few minutes both fleets were mingled, and the admiral ordered us to hoist his flag. At that instant the other ships hoisted French flags, fired on us broadside, and split our main sail.

We were completely confused and taken by surprise. The wind was high, the sea was rough, and not a single one of our guns was ready to be fired. Luckily, the two English ships behind us managed to give the French a broadside as they passed.

Immediately we tossed a lot of things overboard and got our ship ready for fighting. About ten at night we had a new mainsail bent. We wore ship and chased the French, even though they had two more ships than we did. All night and all the next day we pursued them, but we captured only one old India man. After that we headed for the English Channel, and about the close of 1758 we got back safe to England.

Adventures at Sea

It was now between two and three years from when I had first come to England. My master always treated me extremely well, and my attachment and gratitude to him were very great. I was used to being at sea, and I started to feel happy.

I knew Englishmen weren't spirits. I could speak English fairly well. I understood perfectly everything people said. I not only felt at ease with my new countrymen, I enjoyed them. I wanted to resemble them, to drink in their spirit and imitate their manners. I observed and learned everything I could. Every new thing that I saw, I treasured up in my memory.

I never felt half the alarm at any of the numerous dangers I had been in, as I had at my first sight of the Europeans. That fear had been the effect of my ignorance. It wore away as I began to know them.

Everything I had seen on shipboard had combined to make me fearless. I was, in that respect at least, almost an Englishman.

For a long time I had wanted to learn to read and write, but I had made very little progress. When we returned to London, I had my chance. My master had me lodge again with the two sisters, the Miss Guerins, and do small jobs for them. I attended the Miss Guerins on their trips around town. This made me very happy, because I got to see many parts of London. But the best thing was, the Miss Guerins sent me to school.

While I was staying with the Miss Guerins, their servants told me more about Christianity. These servants told me I couldn't go to Heaven unless I was baptized. I believed in a future life, so this worried me. I told the elder Miss Guerin how I felt and asked her if she could have me baptized. My master didn't want that, but she persuaded him to allow it. So in February 1759, with the elder Miss Guerin as my godmother, I was baptized in St. Margaret's Church, Westminster, by the name Gustavus Vassa—the name I have used ever since. I was fourteen years old.

In April the *Namur* was ready for the sea, and my master called me on board. I didn't want to go. I liked my teacher very much. I didn't want to leave London, or school, or the Miss Guerins. But I had to go. The Miss Guerins said good-bye to me and gave me lots of friendly advice and some valuable presents.

The *Namur* sailed to Gibraltar with a large fleet. We got there in eleven days. While we were there, the *Preston* came in. My master said I should soon see my good friend, Dick. But when the *Preston* came in, they told us Dick was dead.

The captain of the *Preston* gave my master Dick's sea chest and all his other things. My master gave them to me. I regarded them as a memorial of my friend whom I loved and grieved for like a brother.

We left Gibraltar and went to Barcelona for provisions. My master, who could speak Spanish and many other languages, was sent on shore to negotiate for provisions. He and I, and some other English officers, stayed on shore, in tents pitched along the bay.

Many Spanish officers used to come to visit my master and talk to him. I didn't know how to ride a horse, so sometimes they would tie me on one so I couldn't fall off and then send the horse out at a full gallop—just for the fun of watching me try to ride.

We went back to sea and fought again off the French coast. Then, while we were in Gibraltar taking on provisions, about seven o'clock one night, we got signals from some frigates: the French fleet was sighted! Immediately we bent our sails, in tremendous hurry and noise and confusion.

Some of our ships went out without their boats, some went out with two captains on board, and some with none. All of us were sailing in the dark.

We sailed all night, and by daylight we saw the sails of seven ships in the distance. About four in the afternoon, we caught up with them. We passed by the whole fleet to attack the eighty-four-gun *Ocean*, the ship of the commander of the fleet. All the other French ships fired at us as we passed them, but our admiral made us lie flat on our bellies on the deck and save our fire for the *Ocean*. When we got quite close to her, all three tiers of our guns fired on her at once.

The *Ocean* immediately returned our fire. The thunder of the guns stunned me and burned many of my companions into eternity.

My station during the engagement was on the middle deck, where I was posted with another boy to bring powder to the aft-most gun.*

*Guns on eighteenth-century ships worked like this. The powder boy brought the gunner one load of powder wrapped in a cloth—that was the cartridge. The gunner rammed the load of powder down the muzzle of the gun with a ramrod, and then rammed a cannonball down the muzzle after it. Then he poured a little powder into a small hole about two inches deep that was on top of the gun, and lit it with a slow-burning wick called a match that was kept lighted in a match tub. In less than a second, the powder in the hole burned down to the big powder charge behind the cannonball. That powder would explode and send the iron ball flying at the enemy. It was important to keep gunpowder away from the match tub because the ships were wooden. If the gunpowder caught fire on the deck, the whole ship could burn up. That's why boys raced to bring powder such a long distance.

At this station my gun-mate and I had a very great risk, for more than half an hour, of blowing up the ship. For when we took the cartridges out of the boxes, the bottoms of many of the cartridges were rotten. Gunpowder ran all over the deck, very near the match tub, and at the end we hardly had enough water to throw on it.

Also we were very much exposed to the enemy's shots. We had to run nearly the whole length of the ship to bring the powder to the guns.

I expected every minute to be my last, especially when I saw our men fall so thick about me. At first I thought it would be better not to go for the powder until after the Frenchmen fired. Then, while they were reloading, I could safely go and come with my powder. But right afterward I thought this precaution was useless. I told myself there was a time set for me to die, as well as to be born.

I cast off all fear or thought of death, and performed all my duties as fast and well as I could. If I survive the battle, I thought, what stories I will have to tell the Miss Guerins!

While I worked I could see many of my companions dashed to pieces and launched into eternity. Shot and splinters flew thick about me. Toward the end of the battle my master was wounded, and I saw him carried down to the surgeon. But though I was much alarmed for him and longed to help him, I dared not leave my post.

At last the French line was broken. We took three prizes, and the rest of the French ships took flight. The *Ocean* and another ship, the *Redoubtable*, tried to escape, but they ran aground at Cape Logas on the east coast of Portugal. The French admiral and some of the crew got ashore. We wanted to get the ships free and take them away as prizes, but we couldn't—so we set fire to them both.

About midnight I saw the *Ocean* blow up. For about a minute the blaze turned the midnight sky into day, with a noise that seemed to tear the world apart.

The *Namur* suffered greatly in the battle. Besides the number of our killed and wounded, the ship itself was almost torn to pieces. All our masts were broken and hung over the side of the ship. We had to get many carpenters from the ships of the fleet to make her ready to sail once more. Afterward we left her admiral to command and, with the prizes, steered for England.

When my master recovered from his wounds, Admiral Boscawen appointed him captain of the *Aetna* fire ship. My master and I left the *Namur* and went on board the *Aetna* at sea. I had a new job. Instead of being a powder boy, I was the captain's steward.

I liked the *Aetna* very much. I was extremely well treated by everyone on board. I had the chance to improve myself by reading and writing, because the captain's clerk taught me. I had practiced my writing a little on the *Namur* too, because there was a school on board.

The *Aetna* joined a large fleet that we thought was going to Cuba, to attack Havana. But about that time the king of England died. I don't know if that was the reason or not, but the expedition was called off. Our ship was stationed at Cowes on the Isle of Wight till the beginning of the year 1761. I went all around the island while we there, and the people were very polite.

One day there, I was walking in a field when I saw a black boy about my size. He had seen me from his master's house, and he was running toward me.

I had never seen him before, and I didn't know what he was doing. At first I was a little afraid, and I tried to get out of his path. But I couldn't avoid him. He came on, straight toward me, and caught me and threw his arms around me just as if I had been his brother.

We became very good friends. I saw him often at his master's house until March 1761, when my master had orders to join an expedition against

Belle Isle, and we went off again in quest of fame.

At Belle Isle, my master landed materials to besiege the French fort. I usually went ashore on the island with him, and one day I got into trouble. I wanted to see how the mortars were fired, so I sneaked past the English sentinel on the shore, and got right up to an English gun battery near the French fort. I saw how the guns worked all right, but I was in tremendous danger from both English and French shells. One of the biggest French shells burst about nine yards from me. If I hadn't dived behind a huge rock, it would have killed me.

I knew I needed to get out of range of the mortars fast. I was a very long way from the ship, and I started to run. Then I saw a French horse. I had a rope with me and used it to make a bridle for him. Then I jumped on his back. Too bad for me! He was not a spirited horse like the horses in Spain. He was the tamest horse I ever rode. Not the shells, not my kicks, not my slaps—nothing would make him run. And every instant I was in danger of dying.

We went a little way, very calmly and slowly, and I met a servant on a good English horse. I cried and told him how badly I needed to escape, and asked for his help.

He did help. With a fine large whip, he lashed

my horse very hard. Suddenly, my horse set off with me at full speed toward the sea. I couldn't stop him or manage him. Faster and faster he ran. The sea quickly got closer, but he did not let up. He was headed straight over a cliff into the ocean!

Just in time, I threw myself off his back and landed on the ground, unhurt. When I got back to the ship, I decided that it was not so good to be fearless.

We took Belle Isle in June. From then to February 1762 we went to Basse-road and block-aded the French fleet. The French tried to break the blockade. Twice they tied fire-floats together with chains. They let the tide float these flaming rafts out among our ships to burn them up, but we sent out boats with grappling hooks and towed them away from the fleet. Sometimes we attacked the French ships with ships of the line, sometimes with boats, and often we took prizes.

In the summer of 1762 we went to Portsmouth for provisions and repairs. In October the ship went to Guernsey. I got to see the old friends I had stayed with when I was first in England, and the little girl, Mary, who had liked me so much.

Then I went back to Portsmouth and the ship. We stayed in the harbor till the end of November, when we began to hear rumors of peace.

BETRAYED!

In the beginning of December 1762, the war was ended. We got orders to go up to London with our ship to be paid off. Besides our salaries, we would each get a share of the prize money—the money the navy would pay us for all the French ships we had captured that they had refitted or sold.

We all cheered and shouted "Huzzah!" when we heard the news of peace. I shared the joy. I was almost seventeen now. All I could think of was being freed, and working for myself, and earning the money to get a good education.

Captain Pascal had not promised me freedom outright, but he had always treated me with the greatest kindness. He even paid attention to my morals. He never let me deceive him, or tell lies. He told me that if I did, God would not love me. Because he always treated me very tenderly, I never thought that he would keep me with him any longer than I wished.

On the *Aetna* there was a man named Daniel Queen, who was also a steward to my master the captain. He taught me how to shave and how to cut hair. We read the Bible together. Many a time we sat up the whole night while I told him of the customs in my country, and how much they were like the customs of the Jews in the Bible.

I loved Daniel Queen almost like a father. When I won money from other boys playing marbles or got some money for shaving someone, I didn't spend it on myself. Instead I'd use it to buy sugar or tobacco for him.

Daniel Queen told me he and I would never part. When our ship was paid off, he said, I would be as free as himself or any other man on board. We would go to London and I could live with him. He would teach me his business, so I could earn a good living.

His promises gave me new life. My heart burned with the desire for freedom. The few days before I gained it seemed so very long!

We sailed from Portsmouth for the Thames and

arrived at Deptford the tenth of December. It was high water, and we cast anchor.

Suddenly a half hour later, my master ordered the barge to be manned. In an instant, he forced me into it.

"You want to leave me!" he shouted down from the deck. "But I will see to it that you don't!"

I was so amazed I couldn't answer him.

Finally I said, "I'll get my books and my chest of clothes."

"I swear you won't move out of my sight!" he said.

He pulled out his saber. "If you move," he said, "I'll cut your throat!"

I began to collect myself and plucked up my courage.

"I am a free man," I responded, "and by law you cannot serve me so!"

But this only enraged him more, and he continued to swear.

"I'll soon let you know whether I can or not!" he shouted, and he sprang into the barge from the ship.

The whole crew watched him with astonishment and sorrow.

Unluckily for me, the tide had just turned out. Quickly it carried us down the river toward the sea, till we came among some ships bound for the West Indies. My master was resolved to put me on board the first vessel he could get to receive me.

The boat's crew pulled against their will. Several times they stopped rowing. They would have rowed to shore, but he would not let them. Some of them tried to cheer me.

"He can't sell you!" they said. "We'll stand by you!"

This revived me a little.

They pulled alongside several ships. Captain Pascal asked them to take me on, but they refused.

I still had hope.

But, just as we had got a little below Gravesend, we came alongside of a ship outward bound on the next tide. She was bound for the West Indies, and her name was the *Charming Sally*; Captain James Doran was in charge of her.

My master went on board to bargain over me. In a little while I was sent for into the cabin.

I went in.

"Do you know me?" Captain Doran asked.

"I do not," I answered.

Said Captain Doran, "You are now my slave."

"My master can't sell me to you or anyone!" I said.

"Why?" said he. "Did not your master buy you?"

I confessed he did. "But I have served him," said I, "for many years, and he has taken all my wages and prize money, for I only got sixpence during the war. Besides this I have been baptized, and by the laws of the land, no man has a right to sell me."

And I added that I had heard a lawyer, and others, at different times tell my master so.

My former master said, "If your prize money had been ten thousand pounds, I had a right to it all, and I would have taken it!"

Captain Doran then said, "The people who tell you he can't sell you are not your friends," and my old master agreed with him.

"It is extraordinary," I said, "that other people don't know the law as well as you."

"You talk too much English!" Captain Doran said. "If you don't behave yourself and be quiet, I have a method bound to make you!"

I knew his power over me. I didn't doubt what he said. I remembered my suffering in the slave ship, and inwardly I shuddered.

"As I cannot get justice among men," I said, "I hope I will in Heaven hereafter."

I immediately left the cabin, filled with resentment and sorrow.

When I came on deck, some of my old shipmates told me not to despair.

"This ship isn't sailing right away," they said. "It will stop in Portsmouth to wait for a convoy. As soon as we get our pay, we'll come to you there. We'll get you back!"

My master soon concluded his bargain with the captain and came out of the cabin to me.

He made me take off my coat, the only one I had with me, and give it to him.

I had about nine guineas with me, all the money I had managed to save in all my years at sea. I hid it that instant, so he wouldn't get that too. It would help me if some way or other I could make my escape to the shore.

The captain and my friends in the crew got into the boat and put off. I followed them with aching eyes as long as I could. When they were out of sight I threw myself on the deck, my heart ready to burst with sorrow and anguish.

HOPES OF RESCUE

I cried very bitterly for some time. Then I began to think I must have done something to displease God—He was punishing me so severely. I thought about my past conduct and remembered something: the morning we arrived in Deptford I had said to myself, "When we reach London, I swear I'll spend the whole day having fun!"

Now my conscience smote me for this casual expression, because I had sworn. I begged God's forgiveness. I prayed for him not to abandon me, nor cast me from his mercy forever.

In a little while my grief was spent with its own violence. It began to subside. My first confusion was over, and I thought with more calmness. I considered that trials and disappointments are sometimes for our good. I thought God might perhaps have permitted this, in order to teach me wisdom and resignation.

These thoughts gave me a little comfort. I got up from the deck with dejection and sorrow in my face, yet with some faint hope that God would deliver me.

Soon afterward, my new master was going on shore. He called me to him.

"Behave yourself," he said, "and do your work as well as the other boys. You will be treated better for it."

I did not answer him.

"Can you swim?" he asked.

I said, "No."

However, I was made to go under the deck, and was carefully watched. The next tide the ship got under way, and soon arrived at the Mother Bank, Portsmouth, where she waited a few days for some of the West India convoy.

The captain was careful to give me no chance of escape. He didn't allow any strange boats to come alongside our ship. When he came up in our boat, it was hoisted immediately.

I tried every means I could devise among the people of the ship to get me a boat from the shore.

A sailor on board took a guinea from me, saying he would get me a boat. Every hour he promised me that it would soon arrive. When he had the watch on deck I watched also, and I looked down the river for hours. It was all in vain. I never saw the boat—or my money.

Still worse, the sailor gave information to the mates. He told them that I wanted to escape, but he never told them he had stolen a guinea from me promising to help me. However, after we had sailed and I told the crew his trick, he was detested and despised by them all.

I was still in hopes that my old shipmates would not forget their promise to come to me in Portsmouth. The day before we sailed, some of them did get to Portsmouth. They sent me some oranges and other presents and sent word that they would come to see me themselves the next day, or the day after.

Also, a lady who had once been very close to my former master sent me a letter. She had always shown me great friendship and had wanted to make me her servant. In her letter she said she would come and take me out of the ship.

However, the next morning the thirtieth of December, 1762, the frigate *Aeolus*, which was to escort the convoy, made the signal for sailing. All the ships raised anchor. Before any of my friends had a chance to help me, our ship got under way.

All my hope was gone! I was a prisoner and could not help myself. I looked back to land, my eyes swimming in tears.

In one day's time, the land was out of sight. I was ready to curse the tide and the wind and even the ship that led us, but the fleet sailed on.

I wished that I had never been born.

LAND OF BONDAGE

The turbulence of my emotions soon gave way to calmer thoughts. I realized that what fate had decreed, no mortal could prevent.

We sailed through calm seas for six weeks, and on the thirteenth of February, 1763, we saw our destined island, Montserrat. At the sight of this land of bondage, horror went through me and chilled my heart. I remembered my former slavery, with its misery, lashings, and chains. I begged God to strike me dead with lightning, rather than to let me be a slave, and sold from lord to lord.

Our ship anchored. I was ordered to help discharge her cargo, loading and unloading the boat, and then I learned what it was to work hard in the scorching West Indian sun. Heavy surf tossed the boat and the people in it so high that sometimes our bones were broken. Every day I was bruised and mangled. And in the midst of my work, two sailors robbed me of all my money, and ran away from the ship.

About the middle of May, the ship would return to England—without me. I could feel fate's blackest clouds gathering over my head. I thought that when they burst, they would mix me with the dead.

One morning Captain Doran sent for me on shore. His messenger told me that my fate was decided.

I came to the captain. He was with Mr. Robert King, a Quaker, and the most important merchant in Montserrat.

"Your master Captain Pascal sent you here to be sold," Captain Doran said, "but he said you were a very deserving boy. He asked me to find the best master possible for you.

"I have seen that you are deserving," the captain added. "If I were going to stay in the West Indies, I would be glad to keep you myself. But I don't dare take you to London. If you get there, you will leave me."

I burst out a-crying and begged him to take me to England, but all to no purpose.

"You will have the very best master in the

whole island of Montserrat," he said. "You'll be as happy with him as you would be in England. I could have sold you to my own brother-in-law for a great deal more money, but just so you'll be happy, I am letting Mr. King have you."

"I've bought you because of your good character," said my new master, Mr. King. "You'll be very well off with me."

He told me he did not live in the West Indies, but in Philadelphia. He was going there soon. Since I understood some arithmetic, when we got there he would put me in school and train me to be a clerk.

This conversation relieved my mind a little. I left these men very thankful to Captain Doran, and even to my old master, Captain Pascal, for the good references they had given me.

I went on board again and said good-bye to all my shipmates. The next day the ship sailed. When it was out of sight, I was so grief-stricken that I couldn't hold up my head for many months. If Mr. King had not been kind to me, I believe I should have died from the grief.

But I soon found out that he was as good a master as Captain Doran had said, for he was very kind. If any of his slaves behaved amiss, he did not beat or mistreat them, he only sold them. This made them afraid of offending him. He treated his slaves better than any man on the island, so he was better and more faithfully served by them in return.

Because of his kind treatment, I finally recovered from my grief and determined to face whatever fate had in store. Mr. King told me he didn't mean to treat me as a common slave and asked me what I could do. I told him I knew something of seamanship, and could shave and cut hair pretty well; I could refine wines, which I had learned on shipboard, where I had often done it; and I could write and understand arithmetic tolerably well.

Mr. King dealt in all kinds of merchandise and kept from one to six clerks. He loaded many vessels in a year, particularly in Philadelphia, where he was born. He had many different-size vessels and doggers that went around the island to collect rum, sugar, and other goods.

I knew how to row boats and manage them well. This hard work was the first that he gave me. In the sugar seasons it was all I did. Sometimes I rowed the boat and slaved at the oars as much as sixteen hours a day. He paid me fifteen pence sterling per day to live on, though sometimes only ten pence. However, this was much more than was allowed to other slaves who used to work often with me.

Those slaves belonged to other gentlemen on

the island. They rented them to Mr. King for three or four shillings a day—but their masters never gave them more than nine pence a day, and seldom more than six pence, to buy their food.

Sometimes, after these slaves had worked all day and their owners had been paid, they refused to give the slaves their share, and flogged them for asking for their pay. Often the slaves were supposed to collect their own four shillings pay for their owners. On Sunday, which was their only free day, the men who had rented them kept them waiting all day long for their pay. Then, when they brought the money to their owners, the owners flogged them for bringing it late.

One slave I knew who delivered his wages the same day, but late, was staked to the ground for his delay, and given fifty lashes.

My master often rented slaves at two and a half shillings per day, and fed the slaves himself. He knew their owners didn't feed them enough for the heavy work they did. These slaves liked my master very much. They worked for him in preference to any man on the island.

Many slaves in Montserrat can't collect their pay at all. They are afraid of being flogged if they return without it, so they run away to whatever shelter they can find. Then their masters put up a reward to bring them in dead or alive. My master in these cases used to bargain with the owners and buy the slaves himself. He saved many of them from a flogging, and in some cases, he may have saved their lives.

In many of the estates where I used to be sent to pick up rum or sugar, they would not deliver it to me, or to any other Negro. Mr. King sent a white man along with me to those places. He used to pay the white man from six to ten shillings a day.

From working like this I saw everything about how the poorest slaves were treated. It reconciled me to my situation and made me bless God for the hands into which I had fallen.

I pleased my master in every job I worked at. Often I worked on board his ships. Sometimes I received and delivered cargoes. Sometimes I delivered goods to stores. Besides that, I shaved Mr. King and fixed his hair, and took care of his horse. He told me that I saved him more than a hundred pounds a year and that I was more useful than any of his white clerks. But his clerks each earned sixty to a hundred pounds a year.

People said that a slave never earns back for his master the money that has been paid for him. This is not even logical. If it were true, why would gentlemen have continued to buy slaves? (The people who claim this of course are the biggest supporters of the slave trade.)

In fact, nothing can be further from the truth. Ninety percent of the skilled labor of the West Indies are Negro slaves, and most earn two dollars a day or even more for their masters. I have known many slaves whose masters would not take a thousand pounds for them.

Various gentlemen who didn't feed or clothe their slaves offered my master 100 guineas for me, but he always told them he would not sell me. Whenever they made an offer I used to double my diligence to avoid getting into their hands. Many of those slave owners used to find fault with my master for feeding his slaves so well. He told them that the slaves looked better well fed and did more work. And yet I often went hungry.

WHAT I WITNESSED

When I was employed by my master, I went to fifteen islands of the West Indies. These are some of the cruelties I saw.

I used to have cargoes of new slaves in my care for sale. The white clerks often abused them terribly, especially the women and girls. Whatever atrocities were done, I had to accept at all times. Such things happened on my master's vessels as well.

One Mr. D— told me he had sold forty-one thousand Negroes, and he once cut off a Negro-man's leg for running away.

"If that man had died in the amputation," I asked, "how could you, as a Christian, answer to God?"

"Answering is a thing of another world," he said. "What I think and do are *policy*."

I reminded him that Jesus taught us "to do unto others as we would that others should do unto us."

He was not ashamed. "What I did worked!" he said. "It cured that man and many others of running away!"

Many slave owners don't live on their estates. The estates are managed by overseers, who treat the field Negroes like animals. They make them sleep in open sheds in damp places, and there they get many diseases.

One Negro-man was half-hanged, and then burned, for attempting to poison a cruel overseer. Repeated cruelties had driven him to despair. Because slaves are human enough to want to end their misery and retaliate against tyrants, they are murdered.

No wonder that in the West Indies it requires twenty-thousand new Negroes annually to fill up the places of the slaves who had died that year.

I saw a Negro beaten once until some of his bones were broken, only for letting a pot boil over.

In several of the islands I saw slaves branded with their master's name, and with a load of heavy iron hooks hung about their necks. Often other instruments of torture were added, like the thumb-screw and the muzzle.

It was not uncommon, after a flogging, to make

slaves go on their knees to their masters and say, "God bless you."

I many times met men slaves who married women of other plantations. They traveled hours to be with them every night. I asked them why they hadn't married one of the women on their own plantation.

They said, "Because when the master or mistress choose to punish the women, they make the husbands flog their wives, and that we could not bear to do."

I saw slaves, especially thin ones, put on scales and weighed, and sold at three pence or six pence a pound. I saw families separated, husbands from wives, children from their parents, to go to work on different islands, and never to see each other again.

And I have seen much more cruelty, much more than this, but if I told you all of it, the catalog would be tedious and disgusting.

Still I do not believe that the dealers in slaves are born worse than other men. It is the slave trade and the greed it brings that hardens men's minds and kills their capacity for kindness. If these same men had taken on another business, they might have been as generous, just, and tender-hearted as they are now unfeeling, rapacious, and cruel.

The slave trade violates the first natural right of mankind—equality and independence. It raises the slave owner to superhuman power, and it lowers the slave to the level of a beast.

And often I wanted to tell the slave-traders—

When you make men slaves, you deprive them of half their virtue. You set them in your own conduct an example of fraud, looting, and cruelty. You steal them and force them to work for you and live with you in a state of war. And then you complain that they are not honest or faithful!

You stupefy them with whippings, and keep them in a state of ignorance. Then you say their minds are so barren that culture would be lost on them.

Why do you use your implements of torture on beings who can reason, just like you? Aren't you ashamed to reduce people just like yourself so low? Above all, don't you see the dangers in what you do, and how every hour you live in dread of vengeance?

But if you give Africans their full human rights, all your fear would vanish. They would be faithful, intelligent, honest, and vigorous, and you would live in prosperity, peace, and happiness.

Some people argue that if slavery is abolished it will be a great loss of money to the economy of

England. I believe the contrary is true. It is in the interest of the manufacturers of England to work for the abolition of slavery. If Africans are allowed to remain in their own countries and trade is established with them, they will exchange cotton and indigo and the still-unknown mineral wealth of Africa for English furniture and clothing and all kinds of English manufactured goods. The abolition of slavery will be a loss to only a few manufacturers—those few persons who now supply the people of Africa with neck yokes, collars, chains, handcuffs, leg bolts, drags, thumbscrews, scourges, iron muzzles, and coffins.

A Glass Tumbler

It was the year 1763, and I was eighteen years old, when I got the chance for a better life.

One of my master's vessels, a Bermudas sloop, about sixty tons burden, carried passengers from island to island. It was commanded by Captain Thomas Farmer, a very alert and active man, who made my master a great deal of money.

Often his sailors used to get drunk and run away from the ship, which hindered his business very much.

Captain Farmer had taken a liking to me. Repeatedly he begged my master to let me make a journey with him as a sailor. Finally my master consented, but he gave Captain Farmer stern instructions not to let me run away. If I did, he said, he would make Captain Farmer pay for me.

I made short trips with the captain and became

so helpful to him that he wanted me with him all the time.

He told my master, "Gustavus is more useful than any three white men!"

And he was right. The white men used to behave badly in many ways. They got drunk a lot. On purpose they would smash the boat that went to shore against rocks—just to delay the next trip and get out of work while the boat was repaired.

My master wanted me on shore, but at last he gave in and gave me my choice of slaving on land or sea. I was very happy at the idea of going to sea. At sea, I might get the chance of earning a little money, or maybe of making my escape. I also expected to get better food, and more of it.

After I had sailed awhile with Captain Farmer I decided to try my skill as a merchant. It was risky. I only had three pence. If I lost that, I would have nothing. But I trusted in the Lord to help me.

I spent the three pence on a glass tumbler. I bought it on the Dutch island of St. Eustatia. On Montserrat I sold it for six pence.

On the next trip I took the six pence and bought two tumblers more. I sold them again on Montserrat for double—a whole shilling. I continued buying and selling like this. In the space of the month I had a dollar. I blessed the Lord that I was so rich.

Then I decided to try for even more money—three times more than I had ever made in any sale.

An old black man was sent by his master to work with us as a sailor. He and I put all our money into oranges, lemons, and limes to sell on the island of Santa Cruz. He bought one bag of fruit. I bought two bags—six shillings'worth, that I knew I could sell for eighteen shillings.

We had just got off the boat in Santa Cruz when two white soldiers came up to us and took our bags of fruit. We thought it was a joke at first—until they didn't give the fruit back.

We followed them down the road, begging for our fruit all the way. They went into a house near the fort and closed the door.

We knocked.

They swore at us.

"Get out of here!" they said. "If you don't leave right now, we'll flog you!"

"This fruit is everything we have!" I said. "We're strangers here. We're from Montserrat. We just came on that ship." And we pointed to it.

But telling them that was a mistake. Now they knew we were strangers, as well as slaves.

They went on swearing and picked up sticks to beat us. Seeing that they meant what they said, we left in the greatest confusion and despair. Instead of having twenty-seven shillings, we had nothing!

I had hoped to make three times more money than I had ever made. Now I would be starting all over again—from nothing. I didn't have a penny.

In our consternation we went to the commander of the fort and told him how his men had treated us. He let loose a volley of curses against us and took out a horse whip. We had to leave the fort, much faster than we had gone in.

In my agony of distress and indignation, I wished that the wrath of God would strike these cruel oppressors dead.

However, we went back to the house and begged again for our fruit. Finally some other people heard us and came out. They asked if we would be content if they kept one bag and gave us back two.

We had no choice. The old man's bag had lemons and oranges mixed, so they kept it, and gave me my two bags.

Immediately I took my bags and ran as fast as I could to get away. My friend stayed behind to plead for his bag. They gave him nothing.

When he caught up with me he cried so bitterly for his loss that I was moved to pity. I gave him one third of my fruit.

We went to the market then, and sold our fruit

uncommonly well: I got thirty-seven bits—$3.70—for my share. Such a strange reversal of fortune made reality seem like a dream. More than ever, I was encouraged to trust in the Lord.

After that, when I had similar problems Captain Farmer took my side and kept many good Christians from robbing me.

THE HORROR OF
THE WEST INDIES

Before I left England I had lived in freedom and plenty. Every place I had ever lived was a paradise compared to the West Indies.

I thought of freedom every hour. If possible, I wanted to get free by honorable means. But I believed that whatever fate had determined would come to pass. If it was my lot to be freed, I should be, no matter how apparently hopeless my situation. If it was not my lot to be freed, I never would be. I prayed to God for my liberty. At the same time, I used every honest means to obtain it.

I went about for four years with Captain Farmer, from one island to another, trading. In that time I became the master of a few pounds, and on my way to making more.

My friendly captain knew about my money. Sometimes it seemed to make him envious, and he treated me angrily.

Every time he did, I told him plainly how I felt. I said that if he didn't treat me well, I wouldn't sail with him. I said that I would die before I was mistreated as other Negroes were. To me, I said, life had no relish when liberty was gone.

I told him this, even though I knew all my hopes of freedom (humanly speaking) depended on him.

But when I threatened him so, he always became mild. He couldn't bear for me to leave him. I took good care of his business and gained him credit with my master. And through his kindness to me, I at last procured my liberty.

So I lived, filled with thoughts of freedom, and resisting bad treatment as well as I was able, and all the time my life was in danger. Every day I faced the devouring fury and howling rage of the surf. Once I saw the surf strike a boat and toss it up on end and cripple several men on board.

Once in the Grenada islands, when I and eight others were rowing a large boat with two puncheons of water in it, a surf hit us. The boat flew with all of us in it, about half a stone's throw. We landed among some trees, far above the high water mark.

At Montserrat one night when we were rowing hard to get offshore, the surf tipped the boat over four times. The first time I very nearly drowned. The jacket I had on kept me above water a little while, and I called out to a man near me, a good swimmer. He caught hold of me and pulled me close enough to shore so I could stand, and then he rescued the boat.

Every day I wished to see my master keep his promise of leaving the West Indies and taking me to Philadelphia.

But while I was dreaming of freedom, a very cruel thing happened that filled me with horror. We were off Montserrat, and a free young mulatto man, Joseph Clipson, was with us. He was a boat-builder. Everyone on the ship knew that he had been free since birth. He had a free woman for a wife, and a child, and a very happy life.

One day a captain from Bermuda and several of his men came on board our ship. The captain told Joseph he wasn't free, and said his master had given him orders to take him away to Bermuda.

Joseph couldn't believe the captain was serious. He showed a certificate of his being born free in St. Kitts, but the captain paid no attention. His men grabbed Joseph and took him out of our ship by force. He asked his captors to take him ashore to a judge, and those infernal invaders of human rights promised him they would. But instead of that, they put him on their ship, and the next day they carried him away. He had no chance for a hearing, no chance to even see his wife or child. Very likely in the rest of his life, he never saw them again.

Before this, I thought only slavery was dreadful, but afterward I thought the life of the free Negro in the West Indies was as bad, or even worse. In the West Indies a free Negro can't give evidence in a court of law. When he is robbed he can't get a hearing in court. And the threat of kidnapping and reenslavement always hangs over his head.

But I was still a slave. If I was caught running away or accused of a crime, anyone could kill me, and never be punished for it. If I was simply slaving as I was supposed to do, anyone could still kill me—paying only the small fine of fifteen pounds for the crime of "bloody-mindedness."

There was a white man once who wanted to steal some pigs I was selling. He came on the ship, refused to pay me, and looked for my money-box to break into and to take my money. To protect my goods and my dignity, I would have hit him and been sent to jail, but a British sailor defended me. The thief went away, swearing the next time he saw me he would kill me and pay the government the fifteen pounds for my life.

I was completely disgusted with the West Indies. From the time I saw Joseph Clipson carried away, I knew I would never be completely free until I left them. In the West Indies, the fear of losing his freedom is always with the free black man.

NAVIGATION.
CHANCES FOR ESCAPE

I decided to make every effort to gain my freedom and to return to England. For this purpose, I decided to learn navigation. I didn't want to run away unless I was ill treated. But if I was ill treated I could take our sloop. It was one of the fastest sailing vessels in the West Indies. I would not have lacked for hands to join me.

I hired the mate of our vessel to teach me navigation. He agreed to do it for twenty-four dollars. I paid him part of the money down. When Captain Farmer found out, he scolded the mate for taking any money from me. But we had so much work that my learning was slow.

A short time later, I had a chance to escape by

signing on a ship bound for France. All the white sailors signed on, and they wanted to take me with them. They swore to protect me if I went. I think I could have got safe to Europe, because their fleet was sailing the very next day. But I remembered the old maxim that honesty is the best policy. Captain Farmer had always been kind to me, so I wouldn't abandon the ship.

He knew I could have escaped too. Out of gratitude for my loyalty, he began to teach me navigation himself. But some of our passengers told him it was a very dangerous thing to teach a Negro navigation, so I was hindered again in my studies.

In 1764 my master bought a larger sloop, called the *Prudence*, and put Captain Farmer in charge of it. We sailed with a load of new slaves to Charleston and Georgia. I brought things to sell there, but I stopped selling them when white men cheated me, as they had in other places.

Luckily, I sold the rest of my goods well when we got back to the West Indies, and so I continued trading during the year 1764.

DESPAIR AND JOY

In 1765 my master fitted out his vessel for a voyage to Philadelphia. I worked doubly hard—loading the ship and buying my own merchandise to take along. I longed to get out of the West Indies. If my master would make good on his original promise to put me in school there and make me a clerk, I would be able to live in Philadelphia.

One Sunday while I was getting ready for the voyage, my master called me to his house.

When I came there I found him and Captain Farmer together.

"I hear that you mean to run away from me when you get to Philadelphia," my master said, "and therefore I must sell you again. You cost me a great deal of money, no less than forty pounds sterling. It will not do to lose so much.

"You are a valuable fellow," he continued. "Any

.

day I can get one hundred guineas for you from many gentlemen on this island."

And then he told me of Captain Doran's brother-in-law, a severe master, who had always wanted to buy me, to make me his overseer.

My captain said, "I could get much more than a hundred guineas for him in Carolina."

I knew that was true. A gentleman had approached Captain Farmer there, and offered to buy me. He had come on board us several times and asked me if I would like to live with him and said he would use me well.

"What work will you put me to?" I had asked.

"You're a sailor," he had said. "I'd make you a captain of one of my rice vessels."

I had sensed a sudden change in Captain Farmer's mood. It had made me afraid he was planning to sell me.

"I won't live with you on any condition!" I had told the gentleman. "If you buy me, I will certainly run away with your ship!"

He had said, "I don't fear that. I would catch you again!" And then he had told me how cruelly he would treat me if I ran away.

"You might not catch Gustavus," Captain Farmer had said. "He knows something about navigation."

To my joy, the gentleman had changed his mind and gone away.

Now I told my master, Mr. King, that I had never said I would run away in Philadelphia.

"I don't even think of it," I said. "You treat me well, and so does the captain. If you had treated me badly, I would have run away long ago."

I explained to him how I saw the world.

"If it is God's will that I ever be freed, it will be so," I said. "If it is not His will, it will not happen."

I told him I hoped that if ever I were freed while I was well treated, it should be by my honest means.

"But I cannot help myself," I said. "You must do as you please. I can only trust in the God of Heaven."

That's what I said—but instantly my mind was big with inventions and full of plans for escape.

Then I appealed to Captain Farmer. "Have you ever seen any sign of my trying to run away?" I asked. "Don't I always come on board when you ask me to?"

I reminded him of the time when all our men deserted the ship at Guadeloupe and went on board the French fleet, and advised me to go with them.

"Don't you know I could have done it?" I asked

him. "Do you think you would ever have got me again?"

The captain's answer was like life to a dead man. To my surprise and great joy, he told my master everything I said was true. He had even set up opportunities for me to escape, he added, to see if I would try to do it, and I never had.

It came out that there was only one reason why my master had thought I would run away: the ship's mate had told him so. I had caught the mate stealing provisions from the ship, and I had told the captain. To get revenge on me, the mate had told my master this lie.

Now everything was clear, and my master instantly changed toward me.

"Gustavus," he said, "you are a sensible fellow! I never did intend to use you as a common slave. I let you go on my ship because I thought you might make money trading. To encourage you, I will let you buy rum and sugar from me on credit, to trade in Philadelphia. If you are careful, in time you will have the money to purchase your freedom. When you are ready, I will let you have it for forty pounds sterling—no more than what I gave for you!"

I was happy beyond measure. "Sir," I said, "I always thought that you would offer me the chance to buy my freedom. It's why I have been so diligent in serving you."

Mr. King then gave me a large piece of silver coin.

The captain told me to go on board ship. He promised that the lying mate would not voyage with him anymore.

This was a change indeed—in the same hour to feel the most exquisite pain and the greatest joy. I was so grateful to both these men that I could have kissed their feet.

I left the room and almost flew to the ship.

THE WISE WOMAN

We soon sailed, and I sold my goods well in the elegant town of Philadelphia.

One day while I was in Philadelphia, I heard about a wise woman and fortune-teller, a Mrs. Davis. People said she revealed secrets and foretold events. I didn't put much faith in this story—but then, the very same night, I dreamed of her!

After that I was as anxious to see her as I had been indifferent before. In the evening when our work was over, I asked the way to her house. When I got there, she came to the door—wearing the very same dress I had seen in my dream!

"You dreamed of me last night," she said. Then she told me many things that had happened to me with a correctness that astonished me.

"You will not be a slave long," she said.

This was very good news. I was more willing to believe it because she had told me the truth about my past.

"Twice in eighteen months," she said, "you will be in very great danger of death. If you live, you will have a good life afterward." She gave me her blessing and we parted.

Our ship returned to the West Indies, where I sold more goods. Then we carried a load of slaves to Georgia. In Georgia I overworked loading the ship. I got a fever and nearly died. I prayed to God to spare me, and promised I would be good if I recovered.

Back in Montserrat we took on more poor oppressed slaves as cargo, and brought them to Charleston, and then to Georgia. While I was in Charleston, there was a great celebration. The whole town was lit up. Guns were fired in salutes, and there were bonfires in the streets and other demonstrations of joy. The Americans were celebrating the news that the Stamp Act would soon be repealed.

In Charleston I sold a white man a puncheon of rum. At first he refused to pay me. Finally he paid me with dollars, but some of them were copper dollars, which were of no value. I went to the market trying to buy things with his copper dollars.

People claimed I was trying to pass counterfeit money. Even though I showed them the man I had got them from, I was within one minute of being tied up and flogged. I ran, and only my own good pair of heels saved me.

We went on to Georgia, which was worse. One Sunday night I was with some Negroes in their master's yard. Their master, one Dr. Perkins, a very severe and cruel man, came in drunk. He didn't like to see any strange Negroes in his yard, so he and a ruffian of a white man he had in his service came at me and beat me with the first weapons they could find.

I cried out as long as I could for help and mercy, but they mangled me and left me nearly dead. I lost so much blood from the wounds I received that I lay numb and motionless. I could not feel anything for many hours. Early in the morning, they took me away to the jail.

After I didn't return to the ship that night, my captain looked for me. He found out I was in the jail and came to me immediately. When he saw me so cut and mangled, he cried.

Soon he got me out of jail to his lodgings, and sent for the best doctors. At first they declared I could never recover. When my captain heard this, he went to all the lawyers in town for their advice, but they told him they could do nothing for me, because I was a Negro.

Then my captain went to Dr. Perkins, the hero who had vanquished me, and challenged him to fight. But cowardice is always the companion of cruelty. The doctor refused.

I was so sore from my wounds that I couldn't rest in any position. The captain nursed me and watched me all night long. Finally, from his care, and the skillfulness of a Dr. Brady, I began to mend. In sixteen days I was able to get out of bed, and do some errands for the captain. After four weeks, I was able to go on duty, and we sailed for Montserrat and stayed there for the rest of the year 1765.

BOXES WITHIN BOXES

Every day now brought me nearer to my freedom. I was impatient to get to sea again, so I could earn enough to purchase it.

In the beginning of the year 1766, my master bought another sloop, the *Nancy*, the largest I had ever seen. My captain chose it for his trips.

This was good for me. The *Nancy* was big enough so that I could carry much more merchandise with me. In Montserrat I had sold four barrels of pork bought in Charleston, and they had earned me a profit of 300 percent. Now that we were sailing in the *Nancy*, I laid in as large a cargo as I could, trusting to God's providence. We set sail for Philadelphia. On this trip I saw whales for the first time, and one puppy whale followed us all day till we got within the Capes.

We arrived safely in Philadelphia. I sold my

goods there chiefly to the Quakers. They never tried to cheat me. Soon I always traded with them in preference to any others.

My sales went very well in Philadelphia. I thought that when we got back to Montserrat, I would sell goods there, and have enough money to buy my freedom. But when we got to the West Indies, we didn't go to Montserrat, and I had no chance to sell anything. We went to St. Eustatia, with orders from the master to sail again immediately to Georgia with more slaves.

When we were back in Savannah, we visited an acquaintance of the captain's, an old silversmith, who was supposed to be very rich. The silversmith said he wanted to return to Montserrat. He pretended to take a liking to Captain Farmer and promised to give him a great deal of money.

While we were loading the *Nancy*, we suddenly got news that the silversmith was sick. In a week's time, he was very bad. The sicker he got, the more he spoke of giving the captain all the money he had promised him.

The old man didn't have a wife or any children—and it looked as if he was going to die. Captain Farmer thought he would inherit all the old man's money and become rich. He took care of him in his illness, day and night.

The captain asked me to wait on the silversmith

too. "When I inherit his property," he said, "I'll give you ten pounds."

I figured that ten pounds would be very useful to me. I already had almost enough to buy my freedom if we got safely back to Montserrat. With ten pounds coming in, I would even have extra.

Expecting my share of the inheritance, I took the money I had and went out shopping. I spent eight pounds on a suit of superfine clothes to dance in at my freedom.

Then I went back to waiting on the silversmith.

We were with him one day till very late at night. We had just gotten back to the ship and to bed, about two in the morning, when the captain was sent for. Someone had come with an urgent message. The silversmith had died.

The captain came to my bed and woke me.

"Get up! Get a light!" he said. "We're going on shore! The old man has died!"

I was very sleepy. "Since he's dead," I said, "he can't want anything. I wish you would let us wait till morning."

"No, no," the captain said, "we'll have the money tonight! I cannot wait till tomorrow—so let us go!"

I got up and struck a light, and away we both went, and saw the man—dead as we could wish.

The captain said he would give him a grand

burial, in gratitude for the promised treasure. He asked for all the belongings of the dead man to be brought forth.

The old man had entrusted the captain with the keys to a nest of trunks. Now the trunks were brought out. With great eagerness and expectation, we opened them. Each one had another inside it. It took forever to get to the smallest. When we opened it, it was full of papers. They looked like bank notes! Our hearts leapt for joy, and the captain clapped his hands and cried out, "Thank God! Here it is!"

But alas, how uncertain and deceitful are all human affairs. We thought we would grasp real substance. Instead the papers were an empty nothing. The whole amount in the nest of trunks was only a dollar and a half—not enough even to pay for the dead man's coffin.

For quite a while the captain and I stood there—ridiculous figures, pictures of chagrin and disappointment.

We went away very disappointed, and left the dead man to do as well as he could for himself—since we had taken such good care of him when he was alive, for nothing.

FREEMAN

We got to Montserrat safely, but still very put out with the dead silversmith. However, after I sold my goods in Montserrat I found I had forty-seven pounds sterling!

I consulted my true friend the captain about how I should go about offering my master the money for my freedom.

"Come to his house Thursday morning," he said. "Mr. King and I will be there at breakfast together."

Accordingly I went there that day. The captain came to meet me, as he had promised.

We went into the room where my master was, and I bowed to him. With my money in my hand and many fears in my heart, I prayed him to be as good as his offer to me.

"You promised me my freedom," I reminded him, "as soon as I could purchase it."

This speech seemed to confound him. He began to recoil, and my heart sank within me.

"What?" he said. "Give you your freedom? Why, where did you get the money? Have you got forty pounds sterling?"

"Yes, sir," I said.

"How did you get it?"

"Very honestly," I said.

"It's true," Captain Farmer said. "Gustavus got the money very honestly—and with much hard work. He is a very careful man."

"He gets money much faster than I do!" said my master. "I would not have made you the promise of freedom, if I had thought you could get the money so soon!"

"Come, Robert," said my friend the captain, clapping my master on the back. "I think you must let him have his freedom. You have laid your money out very well. You have received good interest for it all this time, and here is now the principal at last. I know Gustavus has earned you more than a hundred a year, and he will still save you money, as he will not leave you. Come, Robert, take the money."

"I will not be worse than my promise," said my master. He took the forty pounds sterling and told me to go to the secretary of the Register Office and get my freedom papers drawn up.

These words of my master were like a voice from Heaven to me. In an instant all my fear was turned to bliss, and I bowed with gratitude, unable to express my feelings but with tears, while my true and worthy friend the captain congratulated us both.

Inside I was all tumult, wildness, and delirium. My feet hardly touched the ground. Everyone I met I told of my happiness, and blazed about the virtue of my master and captain.

When I got to the office and told the registrar of my errand, he congratulated me and told me he would draw up my manumission for half-price, a guinea. I thanked him, and with the paper in my hand I returned to my master to get him to sign it, that same day. So before night, I who had been a slave in the morning, trembling at the will of another, was my own master, and completely free. I was twenty-one years old.

That day, the eleventh of July, 1766, was the happiest day I had ever experienced.

After Mr. King signed my paper he said, "We hope you won't leave us, but will stay with the ships."

Out of gratitude to him and Captain Farmer, I agreed. From that day I was entered on board as an able-bodied seaman, at thirty-six shillings per month.

In the streets of Montserrat, all the black people

I met, especially the old people, offered me blessings and prayers.

White and black people both called me by a new name, to me the most desirable in the world—"Freeman."

To share my happiness, I invited all my friends to freedom dances. I danced in my new blue superfine suit from Georgia, and I looked extremely good. Some black women who used to pretend not to notice me began to pay me a lot of attention—but my heart was set on going to London.

Hourly I thought about my old master, Captain Pascal. Despite the way he had treated me, I still loved him. I wanted to surprise him. What would he say when he saw me? I, living where I pleased. I, by God's grace so soon a freeman—not what he would expect, a planter's slave.

I wanted to leave for London immediately, but I had given my word to continue working for Mr. King. A fierce struggle went on inside me, between my inclination and my duty.

How hard it was to keep my word, and how much it would cost me!

A Fight

So I sailed again with my captain, first to the island of St. Eustatia, and then on to Savannah, Georgia. There I went upriver with our boats to get cargo. The river was full of alligators, and they kept trying to get into the boats. If I hadn't shot them, they would have done it. We were very scared of them, but once in Georgia I saw a young one sold alive, for a sixpence.

While we were in Savannah, a slave belonging to a Mr. Read came near our ship and began insulting me. I knew there was little or no law in Georgia to protect a free Negro. It took all the patience I had to do nothing, except ask him to stop.

Instead of taking my advice, he kept on insulting me, and finally he struck me. At that I lost my temper completely and beat him soundly.

The next morning his master, Mr. Read, came to our vessel to talk to me. "I'll have you flogged publicly through all the streets of Savannah for beating my slave!" he said.

I told him the slave had insulted me and provoked the fight by striking me. After he left, I told Captain Farmer and asked him to go to Mr. Read with me to prevent bad consequences.

"Don't worry," said Captain Farmer. "If Mr. Read complains, I'll take care of it. You just go on with your work."

Mr. Read came back and asked the captain to give me to him.

"I don't know anything about this," the captain said. "Gustavus is a freeman."

I was astonished and frightened, and I refused to go with Mr. Read. I thought I had better stay where I was than go be flogged around town without a judge or a jury.

Mr. Read left, swearing he would get a warrant for my arrest and bring all the constables in town to take me off the ship.

I knew he would be back, and I feared a flogging, or worse. I had never borne the welts and open wounds of a flogging on my body—and I dreaded the dishonor of it.

I was a freeman who had done nothing wrong. Yet any white scoundrel could whip me down the streets! Rage seized my soul. I determined to fight the first man who laid hands on me.

"I would rather die like a free man," I thought, "than be scourged by ruffians and have my blood drawn like a slave!"

The captain and my friends tried to reason with

me, to convince me of the danger I was in. I wanted to stand my ground, but finally they persuaded me that I had better leave the ship and hide. I fled to the house outside town where the captain boarded. For five days I was hidden there.

Then my friends told the captain he was treating me badly by not defending me. They told him they were going to get me passage on another vessel.

Right away the captain went to Mr. Read and said he needed my help to load the ship. He begged Mr. Read to forgive me, so that I would come out of hiding.

After much begging, Mr. Read said he wouldn't meddle with me, and I could go to hell, for all he cared.

Captain Farmer came to me right away to tell me how pleasantly matters had gone. He urged me to go back to the ship.

"Did you get the constable's arrest warrant?" my friends asked.

Captain Farmer said no.

"Stay in the house, Gustavus!" they told me. "We'll get you on another ship by evening!"

At that Captain Farmer got almost crazy. He went for the warrant immediately, and finally got it from my hunters—but I had all the expenses to pay.

I LOSE MY FRIEND
AND WIN A NEW TITLE

I thanked my friends for their kindness and went back on board ship, where, as always, there was plenty of work for me to do.

We were in a hurry to get in all the cargo. This time we were taking twenty head of cattle to the West Indies. There, cattle always sold well.

To encourage me in working, the captain promised me that when I got the vessel loaded, I could take two bulls of my own on board. The mate was sick, and I had to do his work as well as my own. When I got the vessel loaded, I asked the captain's permission to load my two bulls.

He said there wasn't room for them. I asked permission to take one. He denied it.

I was very angry at this treatment. I told him I couldn't respect a man who didn't keep his word.

We argued, and I said I would leave the ship.

At that he got dejected, and the mate whose job I was doing advised him to persuade me to stay.

At that the captain said he was sorry for what had gone on. He promised to make everything right when we got to the West Indies, so I agreed to slave on as before.

Soon after that, the oxen came on board. One of them saw the captain and butted him furiously in the chest.

To make up for his broken promise about the oxen, the captain urged me to bring some turkeys on board. He said he would carry all I could find room for.

I told him that I had never carried turkeys and that I thought they were too delicate for a sea journey. But the captain kept urging me to take them. He even said that if they died on the trip, he would pay for them.

I had some paper money that wouldn't be any good in the West Indies. I used it to buy four dozen turkeys, but I was so dissatisfied that I decided I would never voyage to Georgia again, and never again voyage with Captain Farmer.

We set sail for Montserrat. The mate was still sick, and the captain had never recovered from the blow the ox had given him. As the days went by, they both got worse. We met strong northerly winds and rough seas. In a week's time, all the cattle were nearly drowned, and four or five of them died.

The ship was leaking badly. Only seven of us in the crew could work. Every half hour we had to man the pumps to get the water out. The captain and the mate were both too sick to navigate, and I was entirely in charge of the ship. I didn't know how to use a traverse, so I had to steer our course by memory and reasoning only.

The captain worried a lot about the welfare of the ship and the interests of Mr. King. He told me he was very sorry he had never finished teaching me navigation, and swore that if he recovered he would do so.

But in about seventeen days he was so sick he couldn't get out of bed. When he felt he was going to die, he called me to his bedside.

"Gustavus," he asked, "have I ever done you any harm?"

"God forbid I should think so!" I said. "You have been the best of benefactors!"

While I was telling him how much he had done for me, and how I cared for him, he died without saying another word. The next day we committed him to the deep.

All the men on board had loved him, and regretted his death. I didn't know until he was gone how much I had cared for him. Usually he had been mild, generous, and just with me and treated me like a friend and a father. If he had died five months earlier, I don't believe I should have gained my freedom when I did. Maybe I never would have gained it.

The mate came on deck to try to make observations but failed. We got out of the variable winds. I hoped I was steering straight for the island of Antigua, which should be the island closest to us.

In nine days more we got to Antigua, and the day after we got safe to Montserrat.

All the oxen died on the ship, but all my turkeys lived. I sold them at 300 percent profit. I thought their survival through all the bad weather was an instance of God's help to me.

Many people were surprised at my bringing the sloop into port. From that day on, in Montserrat I was called "Captain."

SHIPWRECKED!

Again I wanted to leave for England, but Mr. King begged me to make one more voyage for him. Because of my gratitude to him, I once more agreed.

He named a new captain, William Phillips, to the sloop. We took on a cargo of slaves, and on January 30, 1767, we sailed for Georgia. The new captain strangely boasted of his skill in navigating, and steered a course much farther westward than any navigator I had seen. I thought what he was doing was most extraordinary.

On the fourth of February, which was very soon after we steered our new course, I had a strange dream. I dreamed that the ship was wrecked amid the surf and the rocks and that I was the means of saving everyone on board.

The next night I dreamed the very same dream, but I didn't give much thought to it.

The next night, a little after eight, I was at the end of my watch, and I was pumping water. I was tired after the day's work, and annoyed with the way the ship leaked water.

"Damn the vessel's bottom out!" I swore.

I believed swearing was a sin. Right away my conscience smote me. When I left the deck I went to bed. I had scarcely gone to sleep when I dreamed the same dream as I had dreamed the two preceding nights.

At twelve o'clock the watch was changed. As I always was in charge of the captain's watch, I went up on deck.

At half past one in the morning, the man at the helm saw something under the lee-beam that the vessel washed against. He called to me that there was a grampus and asked me to look at it.

I stood up and observed it for some time. The sea washed over it again and again.

"It's not a fish!" I said. "It's a rock!"

I went down to the captain and told him about the danger we were in, and asked him to come up immediately.

"*It is very well*," he said.

I went up on deck again. A high wind had been protecting us, but now it died down. The current took hold of the ship and carried it sideways toward the rock.

Still the captain did not appear. I went to him again and told him the vessel was near a large rock, and asked him to come with all speed. He said he would.

When I got back on deck, I saw we were not even a pistol shot from the rock, and I heard the noise of the breakers all around us.

I was very alarmed. The captain had still not come on deck.

I ran down to him again, enraged. "Why haven't you come up?" I shouted. "What can you be thinking of! The breakers are all around us, and the vessel is almost on the rock!"

With that, he came on the deck with me, and tried to turn the vessel and get her out of the current, but there wasn't enough wind to do it.

We called all hands on deck and fastened the anchor to a cable. By this time the surf was foaming around us and the breakers made a dreadful noise. We rushed to let the anchor out, hoping it would hold us safe, but just as we let it go, the ship struck the rocks.

Now one swell of the surf followed another, as if each gigantic wave was calling to its fellows. With one single heave forward, the ship was pierced and impaled upon the rocks.

But worse than everything was the thought I had that I was the guilty one. God was punishing me for cursing the vessel on which my life depended. I thought any second we would all go to the bottom of the sea. I determined that if I was saved, I would never curse again. Then, as fast as I could, I started to think of what might save us. My mind was full of inventions and confused with schemes, but I didn't know how we could escape death.

"Nail down the hatches!" the captain ordered. There were twenty slaves in the hold. If the hatches were nailed down, every last one of them would die.

I thought my sin was the cause of the captain's order. If it was obeyed, God would charge me with these people's murder.

This thought rushed on my mind with such violence that I fainted. I recovered just as the crew was about to nail down the hatches.

"Stop!" I said.

"It must be done!" said the captain.

"Why?" I said.

"The boat can carry only ten. If we let them up, they will try to get into it, and we will all drown."

"*You*—" I said, "*you* are the one who deserves to drown! You had no idea how to navigate this vessel!"

I believe, at my least hint of wanting it, the whole crew would have tossed him overboard.

No one nailed down the hatches.

It was still dark then. No one knew where we were, or where to go. We were sure the boat could never survive the surf, so we decided to stay on the dry part of the vessel, and trust to God till daylight appeared.

"We need to get the boat ready for morning," I said.

Some of us began to set about it. Others gave up all concern for the ship or themselves, and started drinking.

Our boat had a piece out of her bottom about two feet long, and we had no materials to mend it. But necessity is the mother of invention. I took some leather from one of the pumps and nailed it over the break, and plastered it over with tallow grease.

So prepared, we waited for daylight. Every minute seemed like an hour till it appeared. When it did, we saw that the surf had subsided and that, five or six miles off, there was a small, desolate island, surrounded by reefs.

We didn't see how our boat could get over the reefs to the island, but we had to get there. We put in only a few provisions so the boat would ride higher on the water, and set off.

Often we all had to get out of the boat, and drag it over the reefs, with our legs getting cut on the rocks. There were only four people who would work with me at the oars—three black men, and a Dutch Creole sailor. We went back and forth from the ship to the island five times that day, without anyone to help us. We made so many journeys, I stripped part of the skin off my hands.

Not one of the white men did anything to preserve their lives. In fact, they soon got so drunk they couldn't have helped if they had tried; and they lay on the deck like swine. Finally, we had to lift them into the boat and carry them on shore by force.

All day we toiled and strained—rowing and hauling as fast as we could, because we were in great danger. If at any time the wind had raised the waves we never could have saved ourselves. At any moment, the leather patch on the boat could have worn out, making it completely useless. Out of thirty-two people we didn't lose one.

I believed that if any one of these people died, God would hold me responsible, which is probably why I worked so hard to save them. Afterward they realized what I had done for them and were grateful, so much so that all the time we were on the island they treated me like their chieftain.

I brought some limes, oranges and lemons on shore; and since the soil was good, I planted some of them as a sign to anyone who would come to the island after us.

When we first saw the island up close, there were some huge birds on it, called flamingos. Because of the reflection of the sun, we thought they were people. Our captain swore they were cannibals. He wanted us to avoid them and to row to another key that was in sight, but at a great distance.

I was against that. If we had had to row so far, we would never have got all the people off the ship.

"Let's go to shore here," I said. "Perhaps these cannibals will take to the water." So we steered toward them. To our joy they walked off, very deliberately. And finally they took flight and relieved us completely of our fears.

Around the island there were turtles, and so many fish that we could catch them without bait. There was also a large rock on the beach that was in the form of a punch bowl on top. When it rained, the rock collected rainwater, which we drank. But if we left it there, in a little while it turned as salty as seawater.

We used sails we had brought from the ship to make tents to live in. Then we started to think how we could get off this uninhabited place. We decided to repair our boat and put to sea to look for a ship, or some inhabited island. It took us eleven days to get the boat ready for the sea, with a sail and other accessories.

Once everything was ready, the captain wanted me to stay on shore, while he went to sea to search for a ship to rescue us all.

I refused. The captain and I and five more set off in the boat, hoping to reach New Providence, one of the Bahama Islands. We had only two musket loads of gunpowder, in case anything should go wrong. For provisions we had only three gallons of rum, four gallons of water, some salt beef, and some biscuits.

On the second day of our voyage we reached Abbico, the largest of the Bahama Islands. All our water was gone, and we were very tired from pulling the oars two days in the heat of the sun.

We hauled the boat ashore to look for water and to spend the night. The island was thickly wooded. We made a fire to ward off wild animals and we hardly slept all night. We didn't find water. The only provision we had left was salt beef. Without water, we couldn't eat it.

All the next day we rowed alongside this island. At night we landed again, and again there was no water. We spent the night just like the previous one, and the next morning we set off again.

We passed several keys, but we didn't meet a ship. Finally we landed on one key. We found some drops of water on some leaves and lapped them up. We dug holes in the sand to look for water, and in one place some thick black stuff came out of the ground. None of us could touch it, except the poor Dutch Creole, who drank about a quart of it.

We tried to catch fish and failed. We were starting to despair. All at once the captain cried out, "A sail! A sail!"

We weren't sure what he saw was a sail, but we got back in the boat and set off after it.

In half an hour we could see for sure that it was a sail. When we came near the ship we saw it was a little sloop, very full of people.

"They are pirates," the captain said, "and they will kill us."

"We must board her," I said, "even if we die for it. If they are pirates, we must fight. Either they die, or we do."

The others immediately agreed. We had two cutlasses and a musket between us, but we were so desperate I believe the captain and I and the Dutch Creole would have fought twenty men.

Quickly we came alongside the sloop and boarded. There were about forty hands on board. How great was our surprise when we found out that most of them were in our predicament!

They belonged to a whaling schooner that was wrecked two days before us. They had left some people on a key, like us, and set off in boats for New Providence to find a ship, when they met this little sloop, called a wrecker, which looks out for wrecks.

In exchange for rescuing the crew, the wrecker would take everything of value on the wreck—and get the crew to help to unload it.

We made this agreement with them, and begged them to go to the key to rescue our people. They did. Everyone on the key was overjoyed to see us, because they had no water.

After some further dangers, we got to New Providence in the Bahamas. We stayed there sixteen or seventeen days. I made many friends there, and met some free black people who were very happy. We passed our time visiting and listening to fiddle music in the shade of the lime and lemon trees.

Finally Captain Phillips hired a sloop to carry him to Georgia with some of the slaves he hadn't sold. A gale sprang up the first day and nearly dashed the sloop against rocks. We got off safely, but some people said someone in Montserrat had put spells on us. Others said it was because we had witches and wizards among the poor helpless slaves.

But I said, "Let us again face the wind and the

seas, and swear not, but trust to God, for He will deliver us."

So we set sail again, and in seven days' time we arrived in Savannah. There I had the usual disagreeable experiences.

A patrol came by a black friend's house, where we were visiting, and said there was a law that any black person who showed a light after nine o'clock at night had to be taken into custody, and either fined or flogged. They didn't take my friend. He was not free, and so he had a master to protect him.

I remembered the limes and lemons in Santa Cruz, and thought what they really wanted was to get money out of me. But nothing satisfied them. They took me to the watchhouse, where early in the morning I saw them flog a Negro man and a Negro woman. Then they said they would flog me.

"I am a free man," I told them. "If there is a law for free men I will have it applied against you." This made them very angry, but finally one of them, more humane than the others, said that since I was free, they shouldn't whip me. Then I sent for Dr. Brady, who had cured me two years before when I was beaten in Savannah. He came to help me, and they let me go.

Another day, a little way out of town, I met two white men.

One of them accosted me and then said to the other, "This is the very fellow we are looking for, that you lost."

The other responded, "I swear he's the one."

With that they came close and were about to grab me.

"Be still and keep off!" I said. "I have seen tricks like this played on other free blacks, but you will not serve me so!"

They hesitated. The first one said to the other, "It will not do."

The other answered, "He speaks too good English."

"I believe I do," I said. "I also have a revengeful stick, equal to the occasion; and my mind is likewise good."

I did not have to use the stick. The rogues quickly left me.

I wanted to get back to Montserrat to see Mr. King, my old master, and then leave the American quarter of the globe. Finally I met a sloop that took me safely to Martinique. There I had a difficulty—the captain of the sloop had borrowed money from me, but when I needed it back he would not return it or give my wages. But finally he did pay me, and I was able to go first to St. Eustatia, and then to St. Kitts.

I wanted to go on to Montserrat, but there was another problem. The captain of the ship going there insisted that I publish an advertisement in a newspaper that I was leaving the island—he didn't want to take the chance that I was an escaping slave!

I thought it was degrading and a gross imposition on a free man to have to place such an advertisement. Besides that, the ship was leaving in the evening—before an advertisement could ever be printed.

At the last moment I found a gentleman I knew who went to the captain with me and swore that I was a free man. The captain accepted his word and took me on board.

A NEW LIFE

On the twenty-third of July, 1767, I arrived in Montserrat.

Immediately I went to see Mr. King, who received me with great friendship. I told him about the wreck of his sloop, the *Nancy*, and what had caused it. I learned with sorrow of his other troubles—while I was gone a flood had washed away most of the town of Plymouth. It had destroyed his home and much of his property, and nearly taken his life.

The good man expressed great affection for me, and was sorry I was leaving him. He urged me to stay in the West Indies. I had a fine reputation, he said, and I would do well there. Soon I would have land and slaves of my own.

I thanked him for his advice and friendship, but said I very much wanted to be in London. I asked him for a letter of reference. Immediately he wrote one out, praising my honesty and my hard work, and gave it to me. With many sincere professions of gratitude and regard, I left him to arrange my departure.

On my last two days in Montserrat, I held free dances with my countrymen, and said farewell to all my friends. On the twenty-sixth of July, 1767, I went on board the ship *Andromache*, and we set sail.

With a light heart I said good-bye—good-bye to the whip and other instruments of torture, good-bye to the angry, howling, dashing surfs— good-bye to Montserrat forever. We were bound for London, the destination I had set for myself so many years before.

I was twenty-two years old. It was eleven years since I had been kidnapped in Africa. As a small, frightened boy I had begun my struggle to obtain this day, the day when I could choose my own life as a free man.

I wished for a thankful heart, to praise the Lord God on high for all his mercies. In my ecstasy, I steered the ship all night.

AFTERWORD

What happened to Olaudah Equiano after he returned to England a free man? He got to London in the fall of 1767 and went to visit his old friends the "Miss Guerins," who were very glad to see him. At their house, he saw Captain Pascal, the old master who had betrayed him.

Olaudah thought that Captain Pascal would be sorry for what he had done—but Captain Pascal was not at all sorry! Olaudah thought of getting justice by suing him in an English court. But because he didn't want to hurt the Miss Guerins, he didn't do it.

He stayed in London and began doing many of the things he had always wanted to do. He hired tutors and went to school. He learned to play the French horn. He became a servant to an English scientist, Dr. Charles Irving, who had developed a method for distilling fresh water from salt water. But Olaudah earned only twelve pounds a year, which was not enough to pay for his studies, so he went back to sea a number of times to make more money. He sailed to France, Turkey, Portugal, Italy, and Spain. In 1773, he sailed with an expedition searching for a northeast passage to India through the Arctic—an expedition that got closer to the North Pole than any ship ever had. Later he sailed to Honduras, made friends among the Miskito Indians—and once again narrowly escaped from men who wanted to re-enslave him.

At the time that Captain Pascal betrayed Olaudah and sold him, he had the legal right to do it. But many English people thought that the law should be changed. In 1771, it was changed: A judge declared that any slave who reached England was free. At that time, there were over 30,000 Africans living in England. Most had been brought to England from the West Indies as slaves. Once they were freed, many of them had no way of earning a living. Some wanted to return to Africa. In 1786, the English Navy hired Olaudah Equiano to be in charge of supplies for three ships that would carry poor Africans back to Africa to establish a colony in Sierra Leone. This job caused him many problems.

He found out that the location of the new free African colony was going to be very near some slave plantations, and he was afraid the Africans making the trip there would be re-enslaved by the plantation owners. He warned the people of the troubles they might face, and many decided not to go.

Then he found that the Englishman who was supposed to have bought all the food and other supplies for the ships was a thief. The man had spent half the money the government provided for supplies and stolen the rest.

Olaudah denounced the man to the government. For doing that, he lost his own job—but in the end the British government praised his work. The free Africans who finally went to Sierra Leone were not re-enslaved, but many of them died there because of the lack of supplies.

Olaudah entered the growing English movement for the abolition of slavery. He presented a petition to the Queen on behalf of the slaves of the West Indies, and he made rich and powerful friends who were opposed to slavery. He wrote his life story, and in 1788, his friends—including English dukes, duchesses, earls, and princes—contributed money so that he could publish it. He traveled all over Ireland, Scotland, and England, making speeches against slavery and selling his book. By 1792, it was a bestseller. It had been published in Russia, Germany, Holland, and the United States. Olaudah Equiano had become England's most influential spokesman for the abolition of slavery.

In 1792, he married an Englishwoman, Susanna Cullen, and they had two daughters. He died in 1797. He was 52 years old.

Slaves on a British ship bound for America, where healthy young men and boys were in great demand. (Library of Congress)

TO BE SOLD on board the Ship *Bance-Island*, on tuesday the 6th of *May* next, at *Ashley-Ferry*, a choice cargo of about 250 fine healthy **NEGROES**, just arrived from the Windward & Rice Coast. —The utmost care has already been taken, and shall be continued, to keep them free from the least danger of being infected with the SMALL-POX, no boat having been on board, and all other communication with people from *Charles-Town* prevented.

Austin, Laurens, & Appleby.

N. B. Full one Half of the above Negroes have had the SMALL-POX in their own Country.

An advertisement announcing the arrival of slaves in the colonies. Families were often divided during these sales. (Bettmann Archives)

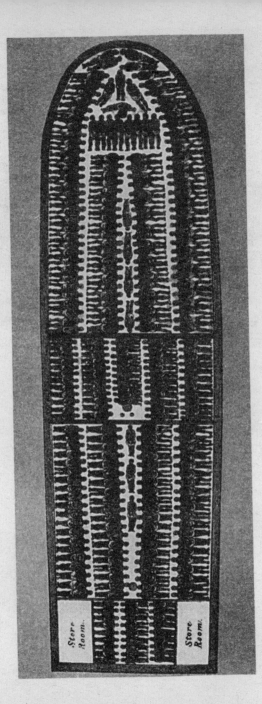

Store
Room.

Store
Room.

Slave traders violently separating a man from his family. (Bettmann Archives)

A diagram showing how slaves were packed into the lower deck of slave ships traveling from Africa. Disease and death were common on board. (Bettmann Archives)

CAPE BRETON

PHILADELPHIA

A VIRGINIA
PLANTATION

CHARLESTON

SAVANNAH

1756

1765-66

1764

MONTSERRAT   BARBADOS

THE TRAVELS OF
OLAUDAH EQUIANO
1755 ~ 1767

1758

1757

1767

1623

1756

LONDON

BARCELONA

GUINEA ● ━━━ ● BENIN

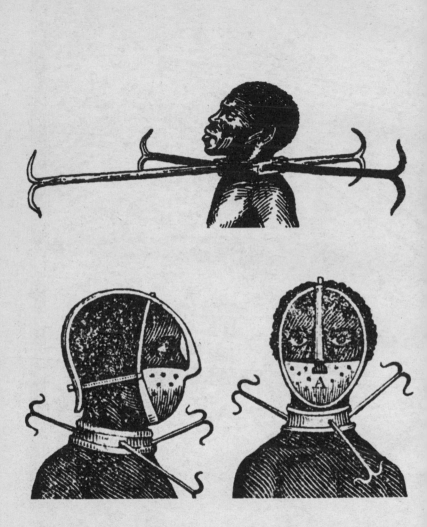

Some of the instruments used to punish slaves and prevent them from escaping. (*top:* William Loren Katz Collection; *bottom:* Library of Congress)

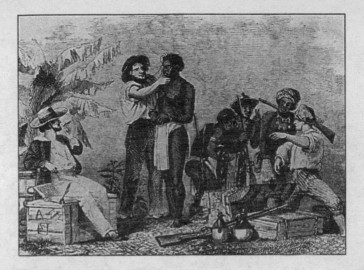

A prospective slave trader inspecting a man in an African port. (Library of Congress)

Africans sometimes sold other Africans into slavery. Here, captured men and women are led to a seaside port for sale to European traders. (New York Public Library Picture Collection)

An engraving by William Blake showing a search for escaped slaves.
(New York Public Library Picture Collection)

NAUTICAL TERMS

Doggers: fishing boats, often with a net for trawling

Fire ship: a vessel loaded with flammable substances and explosives that would be ignited and set adrift to destroy an enemy's ship

Frigate: a heavily armed, fast naval vessel with high sails and one or two gun decks

India man: an English sailing ship carrying goods to and from India

Man-of-war: a warship

Puncheon: a large cask

Traverse: a circular board used in navigation. It was marked with thirty-two radii that represented points on the compass. Each radius had a group of holes for pegs to indicate the number of hours or half hours sailed on each course.

Wear ship: to place a ship at full sail

Windlass: a hoist turned by a crank, used to raise the ship's anchor

---

BIBLIOGRAPHY

Adams, Francis D., comp. *Three Black Writers in Eighteenth-Century England.* Belmont, California: Wadsworth, 1971.

Equiano, Olaudah. *The Life of Olaudah Equiano.* With an introduction by Paul Edwards. London: Dawson's, 1969. (First publication, 1789.)

Gates, Henry Louis, Jr., ed. *The Classic Slave Narratives.* New York: New American Library, 1987.

Platt, Richard. *Stephen Biesty's Cross Sections: Man-of-War.* New York: Dorling Kindersley, 1993.

Stampp, Kenneth. *The Peculiar Institution.* New York: Random House, 1974.

Olaudah Equiano was born to a noble family in the African kingdom of Benin in approximately 1745. While still a boy, he was kidnapped, enslaved, and taken to the West Indies. For the next eleven years he traveled from the Americas to Europe and through the Caribbean. After being freed in 1767, he moved to London, became an active abolitionist, and helped freed slaves settle in the African colony of Sierra Leone. In 1789 he published his best-selling autobiography, *The Interesting Narrative of the Life of Olaudah Equiano, or Gustavus Vassa, the African,* which served as the model for many later writers, including Frederick Douglass. He died in England in 1797, survived by his wife, Susanna Cullen, and their two daughters.

Ann Cameron is the author of many popular books for children, including the best-selling Julian and Hucy chapter books. Her other books include *The Secret Life of Amanda K. Woods* and *The Most Beautiful Place in the World.* Ms. Cameron lives in Guatemala.

THE MOST BEAUTIFUL PLACE IN THE WORLD

by Ann Cameron

Imagine living in the mountains of Guatemala on the shores of a blue lake, surrounded by spectacular volcanoes, bright green fields, and flocks of wild parrots. This is Juan's home.

But Juan's life is less than beautiful. His mother has abandoned him to his grandmother, and Juan must work hard shining shoes to earn his keep. Poor though he is, Juan longs to stop working and attend school. His dream is to learn to read. Can he ever hope to make his grandmother understand?

"A sensitive and compassionate tale."
—*The New York Times Book Review*

"Genuine and touching."
—*The New Yorker*

"A winning choice for reading aloud or alone."
—*The Bulletin of the Center for Children's Books*

**Winner of the Child Study Association Children's Book Award
A Notable Children's Trade Book in the Language Arts**